Pensioners in *Paradis*

French Notes From A Broad

Olga Swan

CROOKED
CAT

Copyright © 2017 byOlga Swan
Cover Design: GoOnWrite.com
All rights reserved.

No part of this book may be used or reproduced in any manner whatsoever without written permission of the author or Crooked Cat Books except for brief quotations used for promotion or in reviews.

First True Cats Non-Fiction Edition, Crooked Cat, 2017

Discover us online:
www.crookedcatbooks.com

Join us on facebook:
www.facebook.com/crookedcat

Tweet a photo of yourself holding
this book to **@crookedcatbooks**
and something nice will happen.

*In memory of Thora,
who always appreciated
the comedy of life.*

About the Author

Olga has a life-long love of writing and language. Her career has included several media appearances, and for five years she was editor of a prize-winning local magazine (c. 3000 subscribers), in which she wrote a regular viewpoint page on local issues and global concerns. For many years Olga lived in France, where she researched her historical works Lamplight and Vichyssoise from original French sources. She likes nothing more than meeting people, reading and researching. Her published books with Crooked Cat have centred on three genres: crime (**3rd Degree Murder**), wartime history (**Lamplight** and **Vichyssoise**) and now the humour, non-fiction genre (**Pensioners in Paradis: French Notes from A Broad.**) In a further guise she has also written for children.

Olga has a B.A. Hons. (Open) in the Humanities, specialising in English language and literature, and self-awarded Honours – gained after six decades of overcoming the rigours of dealing with stupidities and irrelevances everywhere - in the Humanity of Life!

Follow Olga on her weekly blog: olgaswan.blogspot.com, on Facebook and on Twitter @Olgaolgaswan

Acknowledgements

They say that writers should always write about that which they know. Only then will the work that slowly unfolds be readable and realistic. The long hours of research for this novel were, therefore, undertaken in the best reference library possible: my own memory banks.

I should like to thank life itself for the invaluable access it gave me to the inconsistencies, ironies and laugh-out-loud humour which we all encounter from time to time. Whilst the non-fiction work that follows is drawn from a chapter of my own life and that of Him Indoors, the names of the people involved and the place names have been changed to protect the innocent!

Especial thanks go to Laurence and Stephanie, my wonderful publishers and editors at crookedcatbooks.com, for their faith in me. Their indefatigable and never-say-die efforts for all 'Cats' welcomed into their publishing realm are amazing to behold.

Creativity is that indefinable, immaterial entity that doesn't survive without nurturing from those nearest to you. I should therefore like to thank my husband (*aka* Him Indoors) - Monsieur Parody himself - and my family for the support, encouragement and laughter given during the whole writing process. Family is the anchor that pulls writers back into the real world. Never forget them.

Pensioners in *Paradis*

French Notes From A Broad

Contents

PART ONE: AREN'T YOU TOO OLD FOR ALL THIS?

1. In the beginning
2. The pitfalls of house-selling
3. Moving from house to rented accommodation
4. A trip of a lifetime
5. Gendarmes, landladies and weary travellers
6. Searching for that dream French house
7. Back to England
8. In transit: England to France

PART TWO: LA BELLE FRANCE

9. Our new French house
10. We need a French bank account
11. Apéritifs
12. Communication and panic
13. I told you I was ill
14. Bruno.
15. Learning the lingo
16. Renovations
17. Essential requirements
18. It all makes work for the working man to do
19. Un anniversaire
20. Our first visitors
21. Two in a boat (to say nothing of the dog)
22. The market place
23. Pétanque
24. Brocantes fair
25. Size matters
26. Sex à la français
27. Was it all worth it?

Afterword

PART ONE

AREN'T YOU TOO OLD FOR THIS?

1
In the beginning

"It's no disgrace to be poor,
But it might as well be"
Frank McKinney Hubbard

It all started in the suburbs.

High Street was its usual murky self. Poisonous clouds of diesel fumes snaked upwards from apparently eco-friendly municipal buses, their branded livery promising non-stop speedy journeys to the city centre five miles away. Shoppers everywhere played Russian roulette by dodging the traffic, the narrow roads built in another time.

A different mind-set, different way of life.

The buses burped and farted their way through the throng, their speedy design constantly thwarted by those damned other road users. City life everywhere in this crowded island, everyone blindly focused on their own affairs, their own single-minded pursuits.

Pedestrians knew subliminally it was quicker to walk, as they dodged and fought their way along the crowded pavements, narrowly avoiding countless burning fag-ends before tripping over the next shop's illegal pavement sign. Little old ladies everywhere. The same silver-grey perm and trusty tartan shopping-trolley, all barging their way relentlessly down their relentless lives.

Inside the cut-price market hall, curls of tobacco smoke floated ever upwards against the strident tannoy announcements: "Thank you for not smoking."

Past the greasy spoon where the same old dears were busy

spending meagre pensions on curling, streaky bacon, glistening sausage and rubbery egg. Unhealthy? Hah! They had already reached that indefinable age and survived a World War, thank you, so didn't need any sermonizing from patronising do-gooders who thought they knew it all. The very cheek of it!

Every so often, in the style of Julie Walters' Mrs Overall, one of the harassed greasy-spooners would rush out from the back kitchen with a steaming plate, wafting a numbered raffle ticket at the waiting customers sitting with fag-ends drooping: '5 Beans?'

It seemed that all the diseases in the world would walk in through that market hall door, diseases that had been thought extinct long ago, but curiously seemed to linger in the back streets of suburbia. Still alive, still kicking, but hidden away from modern Britain.

All the while, him indoors, whom I have nicknamed 'H', was busy with his market stall, struggling as always to make a living selling DIY.

Have you got a screw loose? Then come and see us, trumpeted his signs.

Well, who else could it be but my other half, with his very own unique sense of humour. You needed it in his line of business. The heaving masses of belligerent Victor Meldrews were always tempted to bring that old broken item, desperate to find someone who understood their old ways. We always thought we were on to a winner targeting pensioners, as there really was a gap in the market for traders who could advise the old and infirm on all those tricky household jobs that their spouse used to do before he passed on. This was something that the burgeoning DIY conglomerates couldn't offer: individual advice and single, small items. But, as usual, we always seemed to miss out. In this case, we never seemed to be able to amass sufficient capital to make a proper go at it. And so we limped along as best we could.

"Where can I find a rubber stopper for my hot-water

bottle?" was a typical refrain from people brought up in a time when things were built to last, and everyone everywhere had to make do and mend – not like the built-in obsolescence of today. So him that knew, in his usual stoical fashion, would reply:

"Look, dear, go and buy yourself a new hot-water bottle. They're only 99p at Bargain Buys over the road."

Many were the requests from the terminally confused for 'candlestick bedspreads', 'Durex batteries', or even: 'Do you know where I can get felt in the market?'

Sometimes people would enquire about neighbouring stalls. One day, a small boy, looking for the pet stall, asked, "Where's the man-eating fish?"

To which would come the quick reply, whilst partaking of his lunch: "Must be his day off. Would you like to see a man eating a cheese sandwich?"

Another boy asked, "Have you got a padlock for a pound?"

"Yes – how big is the pound?" was the quick response.

One busy Saturday afternoon when I courageously opted to help at the shop, I was left aghast as one elderly gentleman, whilst rummaging amongst the multifarious ironmongery, opined to me in all innocence, "You can't get a decent screw anywhere!"

I was constantly impressed by my other half's all-encompassing cheerfulness. As I looked around his tiny emporium, I couldn't help but smile at some of his banners.

Hammers – at knock-down prices!
Buy now before prices saw!
Glue – everything to adhere – but not much more to add here!
Feel free to screwtinise!
Washers direct from the holesalers!
Multipurpose rasps – that won't file a complaint!
Drills make a boring gift!

And the classic sign, propped up against a collection of

dusty ventilation grilles:

Now is the season of our discount vents!

It seemed as if we were embedded, rather like his glue, to the sticky fly-paper of life. No matter how hard we pulled, how hard we tugged, we were stuck there for life. Ever since those early days of our wedded bliss, when we were thrown together into that new maelstrom called marriage, we had fought life's ups and downs with fortitude and humour. We were rather like those Hollywood lovers-to-be whose destinies had become intertwined from the first spark of their chance encounter. William Powell and Carole Lombard on hands and knees at the jeweller's store, their heads bumping together as they searched for that elusive diamond, or John Garfield and Lana Turner, utterly doomed from the very moment of their mingled glance in a roadside eaterie. Would we survive as in all those old Hollywood romances, or would life's harsh repercussions be too much for us?

That night, I watched a documentary on Channel 4, in which a herd of chalk-white Arabian stallions were running wild and free in long, mad, rapturous circles, their white tails carried aloft, then flowing behind them like plumes of silvery smoke. One horse in particular caught my attention. He was tossing his noble head with such arrogance and insouciant pleasure, as if completely possessed by the fluid grace which fashioned and gave force to his galloping forelegs and hindquarters. The glorious abandon and free-flowing mane, all sinewy glossy muscle and speed, evoked something deep within me. With a sudden jolt of realisation, it was clear that everything this horse exhibited with such joy and dynamism was something we lacked, even at our age. We needed to find, before it was too late, the same *joie de vivre* that those horses so unconsciously evinced, but how?

Into the flames of hell.

I suppose the germ of our big adventure started with the

fire. Never could we have imagined, back then in the burgeoning chaos which was shortly to ensue, how, from the ashes of the biggest disaster of our lives, an unimaginable phoenix would rise to push us towards a golden horizon that would change everything – and I mean everything.

It was the summer of 2001 and we were fast asleep at home, dog-tired from the stresses and strains of a never-ending working life. Outside a sudden squall hammered at our windows, but we were scarcely aware of it.

Suddenly there was a hammering on the front door. Groggily, I swam up from the depths and switched on the bedside light to peer myopically at the green digital display on our bedside alarm clock: 4.00 am.

What the hell?

In my usual courageous fashion, I tried to push H out of bed and told him to be sure to fix the chain on the door before seeing who was there at that unearthly hour. Dutifully he struggled out of bed, swearing as he stubbed his toe yet again on the sharp corner of the bed, before stumbling down the stairs.

"All right, all right. I'm coming!" he shouted to the anonymous caller, as he clanged one of his own newly-fitted best brass chain-locks along its narrow, oily channel. He turned the knob and opened the door a crack.

"Oh, it's you," said a ghostly stranger, peering into the shadowy gloom of our inner sanctuary. "Thank God. There's been a fire. Everything's gone. Everything."

"What?" stupidly.

A flicker from the blinking urban street light outside our house illuminated the doorway for a moment. Recognition dawned through the fog of sleep. It was a fellow trader from the shop, looking strange at this hour, out of his usual familiar daytime surroundings. He paused for a moment only to light a cigarette with a nervous, shaking hand. In that instant of illumination, you could see the fingers of his right hand were stained the hue of chestnut from the years of anxiety and stress endemic in a working man's life in these northern climes.

"A fire!" he shouted in increasing volume, as if increased velocity would hammer the message home better than before. "The whole place has gone up. They think it was kids. The police are already there. You'd better come."

Too right we had.

And so began the kind of melodrama that I suppose occurs in most people's lives from time to time. We dashed to the market, sweaters pulled over nightwear, any old socks as they spilled uncompromisingly – as they always do – from the lowest drawer. Why do we always put our vital things in the most difficult to reach spots?

Even if we hadn't known the way to the shop, the smoke would have directed us. All along the familiar route, thick clouds of dirty grey smoke pumped their way ever upwards, above sleeping people's chimneys and moss-covered slippery roof tiles. As we turned into High Street, every belch of smoke signalled the end of our hopes, the finality of our dreams.

The firemen were already there, doing what firemen do. Four gleaming red machines stood proudly in front of the burnt-out shell that used to house our business. Firemen busied themselves with miles of hose, barricading the entrance to all-comers. Even so, we saw at least one wily trader sneak in whilst they weren't looking to retrieve anything of his stock that had survived, wiping the seared and peeling mess off his stock with a greasy sleeve, confident that he could surely still salvage some profit from it.

A local BBC radio vehicle screeched to a halt outside the blackened remains just after our arrival. I agreed to sit in their radio car and give them a personal view – strained with fatigue as I was. I couldn't help but complain about kids today. Why wasn't anyone doing anything about the glut of arson attacks which always seemed to occur during school half-terms? What glee for the kids watching the flames and the excitement of the firemen arriving! And what personal sense of satisfaction to these increasingly street-wise kids, knowing that all incriminating evidence would be destroyed in the ashes of their destruction! I blamed the parents.

Our next thought, after gloomily surveying the scene, was insurance. Of course, they would be sure to pay out, wouldn't they? After all, our policy said we were covered for fire and theft. However – you guessed it – in the end, the answer was No.

They said you have to have evidence of a personal break-in at your individual indoor stall. But, we said, all the evidence is burnt out, and clearly their rule wasn't really appropriate for indoor market halls with one single entry point. Hah! What is it with insurance companies? It makes my blood boil.

You'd be much, much better to put a regular small amount in an account marked 'rainy day', or even under the mattress. At least then it would be always available in emergencies, and you wouldn't have to fill in any stupid forms or answer to anyone.

But the doom and gloom continued. Over the next six months, we lived hand to mouth. However, the market hall owners in their wisdom decided to ignore the advice of all the traders and build something far more up-market than the original dingy but gloriously cheap outlet. Bright lights, gleaming floors, state-of-the-art units with their own personal shutters; no expense was spared. But all this came at a price, pushing up individual rents, thereby pushing up sale prices. It all looked wonderful, of course, and local shoppers came in eagerly at the grand re-opening to peer and wonder at all this splendour. But gradually, month by month, the truth became obvious. The locals had preferred rummaging in the old stalls. They had loved the excitement, the variety and cheapness of it all. It had been like a kaleidoscope of glitter, sparkle and noise, and the customers had loved every bit of it, dodging round each corner for that cut-price bargain that was sure to greet them. But now? Things were just too expensive, but even more than that: the old magic had gone.

Our testing time came in December 2004. It was the end of the mandatory two-year lease and a decision was needed on whether to sign a further one. Eventually, bravely, our answer was the only possible one in the circumstances: No.

Enough was enough. Not only was the business going nowhere; most of our customers seemed to be coming in purely for advice.

"Do you know how to put this together?"

"Did you buy it from me?"

"No – from Bargain Buys over the road."

"Well, then go and ask them."

"They sent me over here to ask you!"

The cheek of it! We sent them off with a flea in their ear.

"Well, if that's your attitude, I won't come in again."

"Good."

Once, when some police officers walked in during their lunch-break from the station a few yards away, H was heard to ask innocently: "Would you like some help with your enquiries…..?"

Things just couldn't go on.

The germ of an idea

That night, over a whisky – well, for H that was – we discussed how to keep him in the style to which he had always been accustomed. Rain was lashing our rotten window frames, whipping soggy flakes of plaster off the sills to lie in a sodden heap on the ground beneath. We just had to get out of here. We were stuck good and fast to the fly-paper, and if we did nothing, life would soon be over.

It was time for lateral thinking.

We mentally stockpiled our assets. For some time, local estate agents had been bombarding us with requests to sell our house. It was detached, with three good-sized bedrooms, on a site of nearly one-third of an acre. There were several excellent schools in the vicinity and a large supermarket at the bottom of the road. Within one hundred yards, there was also a regular bus-route into the city centre. We looked around and realised that we were sitting on a goldmine.

Prices had been steadily rising all over the country and some thought that the prices in our town had reached a peak. It wasn't London but for this area, the value was a good one.

We couldn't believe that anyone would want to pay a quarter million for our house, but apparently that was what it was worth.

"But where are we gonna move to? Wherever we go, the same high prices will still rule the roost." It was him again, ever practical.

"Ah," said I. "I've been thinking..."

"Aggh!" He knew what that meant. It spelt danger, lifting him out of his comfort zone. The transitional phase would mean no more comfy slippers, no more nice, hot dinners.

We were both rapidly heading for pensionerdom, the slippery slope. It would be all uphill now, or should that be a fast route downhill? We couldn't kid ourselves any longer that we could start again in the same old way. Something lateral was required, something we had never ever contemplated before.

You're probably asking yourself: what has she been doing all this time?

Well, for nearly thirty years I had been working as a university administrator. For all its disadvantages – and there were many over the years too numerous to mention – its main attributes to my congenitally-insecure mind were its job stability in uncertain times and its occupational pension. Thank God, back in the good old days of the 1970s, that I had declined the invitation to pay the married woman's stamp. Well, that's not exactly true. I didn't so much decline the invitation; I didn't want to admit that I hadn't a clue what they were on about at the time so blithely told them to stick with the *status quo*.

That accident of fate was the saving grace for these two old fogies now!

So, sitting round the coffee table *chez nous*, we got out a trusty back of an unopened tax demand envelope and grovelled for one of the long-forgotten biros down the back of the settee. There must be a veritable mountain of lost biros and odd coins in that old sofa heaven in the sky. Anyway, at last I found a pen and jotted down some figures.

Every April since time immemorial, my employer had sent

me a glorious pension forecast. Of course, I had always hidden these from H so that he wouldn't feed me the poisonous mushrooms. (What, I hear you say? Seems like a fun guy?) Well, there was an amazing life insurance element of over fifty thousand pounds sterling should anything happen to me whilst still employed. Can you imagine what he would have made of that if he'd only known? But employment had caused me so many headaches over the years.

My mind flew back to what life had been like working under the dreaming spires of higher education. I remembered a time when I had been working there some twenty years – a time of increasing frustration at the lack of promotion possibilities. I knew suddenly that I just had to do all I could to get out. But how? Maybe I could apply for a personal upgrading, so improving my chances a little. I had decided that no longer was I prepared to hit my head on the proverbial glass-ceiling of my job grading. It was drummed into us from the start. It was the jobs that were graded, not the person. So, where was the incentive to improve oneself? Good, bad or indifferent, we were all lumped together in the grade that went with the job. So, to succeed with a personal upgrading application, it was necessary to show that the job itself had become more sophisticated, not me, even though it was undoubtedly me who had made the job more diverse in the first place!

Following my application, I was called in front of the full university grading committee, housed in the formal Senate Room. I was called in, like a lamb to the slaughter, to find myself sitting at an enormous oval table, the sort you would expect to find in the White House, in front of seven people! I almost expected the chairman to be wearing one of those black caps that the hanging judges of old used to wear. My application was read out, then the chairman asked me whether I wished to say anything in mitigation in my defence. I could only sit, quaking in my boots, dumbly submissive in front of such austere surroundings.

My eyes wandered around the enormous room, taking in

the expensive oil paintings of past Chancellors of this prestigious institution. Whichever way I looked, their dark eyes seemed to follow me in abject disapproval at such a lowly person being ensconced in their eminent presence. The chairman turned to the three persons on his right, apparently union members who were supposed to be on my side. Three ayes. My hopes rose. He turned to the elderly gentlemen on his left. Three shakes of the head. The chairman stroked his grey beard and pronounced that, in the circumstances, he as chairman was allowed a casting vote.

The large expensive clock on the wall ticked on solemnly awaiting the decisive verdict. In the sudden cool of the room, I felt sweat chill like rime on my skin.

In life there are often unexpected comedy moments, amidst the most serious situations. Whilst all waited with ba

ted breath, into the room clanked the wheels of a tea-trolley, followed by an elderly lady in large apron.

The chairman glanced up in irritation, and said, "Not now, Gladys, not now!"

Gladys clanked out again in a huff, banging the door behind her.

Eventually, his mind evidently made up, the chairman pronounced his decision.

"As you know, I am allowed a casting vote in such circumstances as this…"

"Yes, yes, get on with it."

"…but in this case I have decided not to exercise my vote." His eyes looked downwards, not wanting to meet my incredulous expression.

Everyone looked stunned.

"What does that mean?" I asked one of the union members. He looked miserable.

"It means that, because the decision is tied, your grading stays as it is."

I couldn't believe it. After all that, I was back where I started. My nervousness turned to rage. I stormed out and ran down the curved, ornate stairs. Outside the Vice-Chancellor's suite at the foot of the stairs, I couldn't help but notice that workmen were just completing what looked like very expensive refurbishments to the whole suite. They were laying rich, deep Indian carpets as a backdrop to the heavy mahogany furniture and gilt table ornaments. That just rubbed salt into my wounds. I had just been denied what would have amounted to a measly five hundred pounds more a year, after having worked there for some twenty years, only to be confronted by work costing thousands!

Clearly, appearances were all important in the world of higher education. Forget the staff who do all the daily work. The world of spin is everywhere: all you have to do to get anywhere in this world is give an *appearance* of worth. I glanced in a small mirror in the corridor. Middle-aged woman running to fat, hair awry and eyes blazing. There's your answer, then.

An old professor, glorious in his wisdom, once told me: only fight the battles you've got a chance of winning. Well, it was clear that after all these years, I had little chance of winning this particular battle. So I took him at his word. There was clearly only one way out.

I emerged from the flatulent warmth of the detested gleaming spires, mind reeling and onto the sunny campus with its sprawling rectangles of springy green grass, its crowd of laughing students, canopied trees and rainbow-bright flower-beds. I sat down for a moment to still my racing blood pressure and calm my nerves. I looked down and saw that a large black beetle had somehow found himself on his back, tiny legs frantically waving in the air in his efforts to right himself again. I picked up a nearby stick and gently turned him over. He paused a moment as if not believing that the hand of God had somehow given him his life back again, before scuttling off on his beetly business again. Perhaps all this was telling me something. If only I could find a way of extricating myself, maybe there was a golden path ahead.

I shook my head clear of my conjectures. There was no point on mulling on past disasters. It was time to look to the future.

Next Monday, as the local train whistled past, I thought of all those commuters on their daily grind. I fixed my eyes on one particularly harassed person as her image flashed by, willing my thoughts directly to her. Are you on the commuter train on your way to yet another worrying working day? As the wheels clack beneath you in their familiar Monday morning rhythm and the urban lifestyle whistles past on its daily grind, sit back and close your eyes a moment. What have you achieved in your busy life? Yes, you may have a nice home, wide-screen TV, smart car maybe but inevitably all of these came at a cost. Undoubtedly, unless you've won the lottery, you will be saddled with a large mortgage, loans and credit cards but doesn't everybody? Maybe you are in your fifties, like me, but couldn't possible retire yet as early-retirement means you would have to live on the inevitably reduced pension provided by your pension scheme. Could it be that all your hard-won assets, apart from your spouse and family, are mere material possessions required by the urban environment you chose to live in — that you are merely working to live and living to work? That was certainly how I felt just at that moment and something drastic just had to be done. I shook my head of these thoughts and concentrated again on our own problems.

Back around the coffee table, H and I peered closely at the figures again on the envelope.

Needing to clear my head, I rose to open the window wide, letting a small fresh breeze bend and shake the prickly hawthorn bush under the window and filling the room with the sound of splashing rain, before returning to the table again.

"This is no good," my other half said. "It says you can only get your work pension when you're sixty-five, and that's years away yet..." Head sunk in dismay. Bottle of pills at the ready.

But wait. There's an avenue of opportunity. Looking closer, it became apparent that after the age of fifty, you could request special dispensation to claim a smaller pension right away. In fact, the previous quarter's university bulletin had boldly proclaimed that all departments were now actively encouraging their over-fifties to do just that. After all, why would any employer want to keep people who had built up a lifetime of knowledge and expertise? Why would any university want to keep people who were constantly in demand from students and staff alike, who regularly picked their brains for lifelong snippets of wisdom gleaned from the streets of life? Far better to bring in new shiny suits, fresh from school, who knew sod-all, and pay them just the same as you.

What was it Confucius always said? In times of confusion, bring in lots of new people and reorganise everything. That way everyone thinks that things are getting done, but in truth, it merely keeps people busy whilst the essential things remain the same.

As the rain finally cleared outside, filling the room with a sudden glimmer of dusky light, H and I got our heads together and made a plan of action.

First, keep calm.

We wrote down the annual university pension amount if I were to leave in, say, six months.

Too low! We can't live on that. But, wait a minute. What did that estate agent say our house was worth? We wrote down that magical quarter of a million. But what about the business debts? And there's still a small mortgage left. Time to get technical. We drew a line down the envelope and started totting up what must be paid to that dratted bank manager, worked out the quoted one percent of sale price for the estate agent, likely solicitor fees, the precise amount to pay off the rest of our tiny mortgage, etc. etc.

"But," moaned H. "Where are we gonna live?"

"Ah," said I. "I have a plan."

"Aargh!"

"Now you're sure you're gonna listen?" said I. I took the shake of his head for assent before blithely continuing.

"I've been looking at property prices in southern France, in my lunch hour…"

"What!"

"No, really. It's amazing what you can find on the Internet... I know, you're not supposed to do that at work, but nothing ventured, nothing gained. After all, what could they do — sack me? I was leaving anyway. Look, if we were to move to France we could pick up a house for less than half of what we get for our house here..."

"But what we gonna live on? We've agreed your work pension is too low. I can't speak French. How am I gonna get a job over there...?" Him indoors again.

"That's just it. We won't have to. Don't you see? With the money left over after buying a cheap house in France and paying off all our debts, the bank interest plus my University pension might just do. And the beauty of my plan is, we could go now, and then when I reach sixty, there'll be an extra four thousand or so a year to look forward to from the Chancellor, followed by your State pension when you get to sixty-five."

"But that's not fair. Why should you get your State pension at sixty, and I've got to wait another five years...?"

"You haven't been listening to a word I've been saying. You should be thanking your lucky stars that I was born just before 1950 and so still qualify to retire at sixty. I've been doing my research. If we move to anywhere in the EU, our state pensions will be index-linked. If we'd decided to move to Canada, Australia or South Africa, instead, our pensions would be frozen from the point when we first collect them. Just think. If we move to the south of France, not only will our income increase each year, the weather should mean lower heating bills too. The plan's perfect!"

I jumped up and down in excitement. He reached for the envelope again and the whisky in alternating surges. Then he grabbed his reading glasses, polishing off yesterday's dinner stains with the edge of his shirt. I waited whilst he absorbed my grand plan.

The seconds ticked by.

He knew from years of long-sufferance. Once my mind was made up...

21

Eventually, heralded by a grunt, "But if this plan is so foolproof, why isn't everyone doing it?"

Another local train chugged past and I thought of all those daily commuters again. Let me take you to another world, a world where the view outside your window is no longer congested by rushing people and choked by cars and buildings that always seem to be grander and more affluent than yours, to a green, rural and idyllic scene. It is a world where you no longer have to rush out to work on yet another dash to the office, but one where you have time to 'stand and stare.' There are luscious fruits and cost-saving vegetables to be grown in your own grounds — land which is big enough to provide privacy and space for you and your family on this God-given earth. Every so often, you can take a breather, lean on the fence and watch the sheep and goats running freely in the fields beyond your borders. You look up at the luminous sky and see a blueness and clarity of light that you had forgotten even existed. Gone are the grey days and ever-changing winds of a northern climate, replaced at last by long warm summers, picnics and walks with the dogs by the riverside.

As if to reassure myself, I convinced myself that the achievement of this miracle is not difficult. All that is required is a re-evaluation of your life and goals. In your new idyllic world, you would no longer have to view prospective houses with an English eye, but with a balanced viewpoint based on the values of your new community. If your new neighbours do not require all your previously *essential* material possessions, then in future neither do you. Once this notion has taken root, anything is possible.

Looking back at H, I could only spread my hands and shrug in response.

Je ne suis pas le bon dieu!

2
The pitfalls of house selling

The house is for sale.

It says so on the brand new sales board sprouting proudly and somewhat drunkenly to the right at the front of the hedge.

Rule number one: make sure the house looks smarter than the sign. I'd been watching all those TV programmes avidly and knew that it was a fate worse than death to have both the exterior and interior looking anything but immaculate when that unforeseen buyer walks up the drive.

But how to do that?

We were no longer young and were both still working every day. But needs must. So, cleaning and throwing out began in earnest. What seemed perfectly comfortable and presentable to us old fogies clearly wouldn't do for that smart young couple who were going to come to view. Him indoors was sent outside to neaten up the front hedge and garden. I told him this was no time to unleash all his aches and pains. If a job was worth doing…..

Day followed relentless day until, with a sigh of relief, I surveyed the scene with some feeling of contentment. Yes, it might just do. I'd painted over the patches of black mould on the third bedroom wall, and emulsioned everywhere in that pleasingly bland style that TV presenters loved. Typically, on seeing me with paint pot in hand, him indoors opined "Don't get carried away with emulsion…."

"I'll gloss over that." Oh no, it's getting to me too.

I'd tried to think of everything. I had even obtained a can of fragrant fabric freshener to use just as that elusive purchaser walked up the drive.

The following morning the estate agent rang. Would 5:30 be convenient for our first viewing? "Of course," I replied blithely, "no problem." I put the phone down.

"Aargh."

But at least it was a time before him indoors came home to mess the carpet up with his muddy feet. That was something at least. That evening I managed to leave work early and rushed home. I hurriedly stuffed things into cupboards and under beds. At least the weather was fine, so I was able to open the patio doors and bring a little fresh air into the room. Someone once told me: "if you're in a rush and haven't got time to clean the whole house before an impending visit, clean the windows and spruce up the kitchen and bathroom. Even if the room's untidy, the clean windows will make everything look clean. And it's vital to keep the kitchen and bathroom clean and immaculate."

After that I just had time to pop the coffee percolator on, tune the radio low to Classic FM, and spray fabric freshener on the wallpaper opposite the front door, and on the curtains and furniture in the lounge.

Ding-dong.

Phew, just finished in time. I dusted my sweating hands on the back of my jeans, smoothed my hair, and nonchalantly opened the door. My first surprise was seeing a man hobbling towards me on crutches, guided by what appeared to be his two children. Second surprise was recognising him as a neighbour from up the road. Inwardly I knew what him indoors would say if they bought it: "We needn't have employed an estate agents; we could have merely put our own home-made sign up and saved all those estate agent fees." But there was no point in thinking about that now. I turned my head and smiled at our viewer as he hobbled in.

"Sorry about the crutches. I cracked a bone in my foot playing football…"

"Oh, that's O.K. Please come in, come in," blithely ushering the ungainly contingent along the narrow hall towards the lounge, wondering how on earth he was going to get upstairs….

"This is the lounge," unnecessarily, quickly glancing around to reassure me that all was in place. The carpet had been vacuumed, the furniture plumped up, and the pictures on the wall appeared to be sitting square.

As all newcomers seem to do, he hardly noticed his surroundings, just glancing here and there before manoeuvring himself towards the windows and looking out at the view. "Ah, this is nice. Much better than our house up the road. It's so peaceful here, isn't it?"

"Oh yes," I replied, bottling in inner anxieties that the noisy family two doors away wouldn't make their usual commotion until after the viewing was over. As he poked and prodded his way back along the hall and into the large kitchen, I rehearsed the spiel I had suddenly devised.

Noting he said he had need of a lot of space because of his large family, I blithely opined: "I've always said that the most important thing in a house is that all the family need space to sit and eat around a large table in the kitchen. Here there is plenty of room for mother to cook lots of noodles and rice on this large hob and she can serve it hot directly to all your relatives sitting round the table. Just think: she won't miss out on any of the news and family gossip…"

"Yes, yes," he said thoughtfully, as he turned and looked carefully around. "Will you be leaving all these appliances?" shrewdly.

"Yes. You won't have to buy anything new. You've got all you need. There's a dishwasher, washing machine and even a deep fat fryer for the kids' chips…." Steady girl, I thought to myself. Don't overdo it. We had decided that there was no point in trying to take any of these appliances with us. In any case, they were all built-I, ancient and would be too difficult to extricate.

As we came out of the kitchen, I asked him how he was going to view the upstairs.

"I'll send my eldest," pointing to his eleven-year old boy. "He knows what to look for. And I'll trust his judgement." Seemed a bit strange to me but I wasn't about to argue.

As the boy scooted upstairs, I called after him stupidly,

"don't forget to note the extra large washbasin in the bathroom — you could bath the baby in there…" I chided myself. There you go again, overdoing things. My eyes focused on my keyring lying on the hall table. It had my name on the front, with words stencilled on the back: "She always overdoes things and does more than she is asked." I couldn't believe how true that was for me.

Soon, it was time for them to leave. They did seem very impressed. I was convinced of it.

Sure enough, the next day, Sue, our estate agent, was on the phone.

"You've had your first offer."

"I knew it," gleefully.

"But, I'm afraid it's rather less than you'd hoped…"

"How much?" eagerly.

"Well, your viewer yesterday has offered two hundred and twenty thousand…"

"What? But that's thirty thousand less than we're asking…"

"I know. It does seem rather low, I must admit… But still, it's a difficult market at the moment."

"No. Definitely not. We wouldn't even consider such a low offer. It's an insult."

And so the viewings continued. I even fell into a pattern, wielding my fabric freshener, coffee percolator and highbrow music to something reaching sublime perfection. But after the first week, the viewings fell off a little and we still had only that one derisory offer.

I started to panic. That night, I spoke to him indoors again.

"What are we gonna do? It doesn't look as if we're gonna get our advertised asking price."

"But you said that we had to have that if we're gonna make a go of our plans."

"I know, but…"

"Aargh."

"I know what you're gonna say, but I've been looking at the figures again. Maybe, it might just be O.K. if we accepted a bit less than the asking price."

"Just how much less exactly?"

"Well, I was thinking we could go back to our first caller and say that, although two hundred and twenty thousand was still too low for us, we could consider two hundred and thirty…"

"Are you sure? I mean, will we have enough then to live on in France?"

"I think so. It just means we'll have to pull in our belts a little tighter."

"Mine's already at its tightest notch already," studying his increasing paunch, evidence of too many lunches at the greasy spoon and the now daily pint at the Red Lion next door.

Outside a typical English summer was hammering loudly against the windows, the rain running in cold rivulets to collect in damp puddles on the still rotting windowsills beneath.

Damn. I'll need to varnish over those sills yet again tomorrow.

I knew that you were supposed to do the job right and use a sander first, but I couldn't cope with it all. I was constantly looking for the quick fix. I just couldn't relax whilst the house remained unsold.

My eyes settled on the coffee table. I flipped open some of the various books I'd been collecting as research for our future.

"*Are you sure you're making the right choice?*" they all seemed to shout out from their glossy pages.

"*You need to be brutally honest with yourself, your partner and everyone else in the family about what you are contemplating. Why are you doing this? What do you expect from your new life abroad? To make it happen, there are a number of things you will need to put into practice: research, planning and a very well-developed sense of humour…*"

Well, looking at my other half, the last item was certainly well-established. According to his father, he had already been making the other kids laugh in school over forty years ago.

"The teacher said: sit down for the present, but I never got one."

"On leaving school for the last time, the Head said to him: it gives me great pleasure to turn out a boy like you. I only wish I'd done it five years earlier."

It was clearly a congenital malady.

Suddenly we were surprised out of our musings by an unexpected knocking at the door. We looked at each other, each asking the same thing. There was only one way to find out. I jumped up, stuffing various newspapers and magazines under the cushions of the sofa, and rushed to the front door. I took a deep breath and turned the knob.

"Hello. Hope you don't mind, but we so liked your house that we wanted to take another look."

It was the man with the offer, minus his crutches and minus his children.

"Yes, yes, of course," abstractedly ushering him in.

Didn't have time for the fabric freshener. Oh well...

The two men shook hands and I realised that this was a bonus. Men in these situations always relate better to other men. Traditional practices of gentlemanly agreements over cigars crowded into my mind. Yes, maybe this time it would be better, as long as he laid off the jokes....

By the time I'd recovered my senses, him indoors was talking politely about all those things that I didn't know anything about: the cricket at Edgbaston, the delights of the potting shed, the different types of trees in our back garden, etc. He had already ushered our guest through the patio doors onto the back terrace and was pointing out the quality of the pointing (!) on the roof and the fact that there were no slates missing.

"Yes," he was saying when I joined them. "You can always tell the quality of a house by the state of the brickwork and roof tiles at the back."

Clever, I thought. *Very clever.* He knew, as did I, that the back view of the house was far better than the front elevation with its flaky and rotting window sills.

"Yes, I see," said our prospective buyer thoughtfully. "Yes, you're absolutely right."

"And," my other half continued, "there is plenty of scope for building an extension on the left there, over the garage. That way you could include a further bedroom and maybe an en-suite too."

Clearly I had underestimated him.

I could see our buyer mulling over the space he so evidently needed for his family.

After a further wander around the garden and an appreciative glance at the high, private fencing all around, we ambled deceptively casually back into the house.

"I'm pleased to see that your foot's now better," I said in pleasant conversational mode.

"Oh yes, so am I. I can't tell you how difficult it's been trying to view houses when you can't even go upstairs…"

Like all women in these kind of unexpected situations, my mind flicked to the likely scene upstairs. Yes, I thought with relief. It should look O.K. I did it just this morning.

"Would you like to take a look now?" casually.

"Yes please. I know my son told me about it, but you can't really tell properly until you've seen it for yourself."

No, indeed.

But all went well. He was suitably impressed with our highlights: the extra-large washbasin, the light sunny bedrooms, and I managed to position myself right in front of the wall where I had emulsioned over the black mould, shielding the worst of it. We made our way down the winding staircase, the one that is so difficult to manoeuvre beds up and down.

"This is a particular character feature," I pointed out with one hand elegantly gracing the mahogany handrail. "You don't find a dog-leg staircase in every home."

"No indeed," he replied puzzled.

We walked back into the lounge and I ushered him into our best armchair.

I made coffee, handing out our best china cups, and we started to discuss the nitty-gritty.

Well, to cut a long story short, we finally shook hands on

his offer of two hundred and thirty-thousand pounds. He ummed and ahed a bit, saying he would need to get business loans from various uncles to fully finance the deal, but at last it was settled. We waved goodbyes at the door, promising to sort out the final details without delay. The two of us returned to the lounge with euphoria, but with feelings of no little trepidation.

We had actually sold the house!

3
Moving from house to rented accommodation

It's now October and the leaves are slowly turning into wonderful autumnal hues before they lie crushed and broken underfoot. I hoped that that wasn't an omen for the future.

Stop it! No time for depression. This isn't the season of our discontent (sic) but the season of our wonderful and glorious future.

There's been a big change in him indoors. His whole attitude is starting to change from one of absolute disbelief to one of steadily rising expectation. And me? My attitude has been marked by steadily-rising hysteria. Of course, to friends, family and work colleagues I blithely recount how, yes, we've just sold our house and then we'll rent a while whilst we look further afield. But inside, I'm like the proverbial duck: calm and unruffled on the surface, whilst flapping frantically like the clappers underneath the surface.

It was ever so.

But things are now definitely moving on. I've found a furnished flat that should keep him indoors temporarily in the style to which he's been accustomed, whilst meeting my stringent budget requirements.

Here's the plan. We rent for six months, during which time I shall continue to work — a necessity in order to pay the rent! And we fail to renew the lease on the business. Early in the new year, at the start of a new quota of holiday leave days, I shall take two weeks from work so that the two of us can drive down to the south of France to begin our house hunting in earnest. Then, once we've secured a property, we return to our English flat, and a month before the end of the rental period, I hand in my notice at work.

No stress then!

First, down to brass tacks. We ruthlessly sort our furnishings, belongings and all effects into three containers. Well, I'm being ruthless, whilst he keeps saying: "No, you can't throw that out, I need it!"

Typical. At this rate, we won't be throwing anything out.

Anyway, essentially the skip will be for rubbish we won't need (no, I need H for all that grass-cutting!); the second container will be for everything to put in store, that is stuff we intend to take with us to France, and the third pile will be for small items we will need to take to the furnished flat to tide us over for the next six months.

As the big moving day nears, in other words when our solicitor finally pulls his finger out and gets that all-important cheque in our bank account, we start to progress plans into finer detail. Sometimes in life fate takes a hand, and this was the case here. As luck would have it, Sue, our estate agent was chatting to me and asked where we were moving to.

"Oh, somewhere in the south of France, but we don't really know where yet. We want it to be south so that we can benefit from the sunshine, but not near the coast as the property prices are too high there, nor in Spain because neither of us speaks any Spanish. I can muster sufficient French to get by, so felt that was the most important thing really. I don't think I could contemplate moving anywhere without speaking the language."

"No, you're absolutely right," reassured Sue. "Look, why don't you talk to our agent in that region? He's originally from England and is coming up to the Midlands next week for the International Property Show at the NEC. He has his own agency in SW France. Would you like me to set up a meeting with him?"

"Wow. What a stroke of luck. Yes, that would be great. We were kind of thinking of that area because really, from searching through the Internet, property prices in the south-west, inland areas look to be much more within budget."

"Yes, I agree with you. His agency is set in a tiny

mediaeval village where rural property is still relatively cheap. It sounds as though that area might be just what you're looking for."

Things now took on a momentum all their own. Him indoors still had plenty of material to fuel his peculiar sense of humour, and I developed more grey hairs with every day that passed.

It was now January. There was an impressive cheque sitting in our bank account, the numbers of which we kept running our fingers over to see if really true. After finally paying off all our business debts, we had great pleasure in telling the bank manager exactly what he could do with our now defunct business account. We recalled only too well his past attitude to us, as we sat meekly subdued and intimidated in his lordly presence. How many times had we rushed in with cash-bag slung hastily around our waist asking for change, only to be told that that would incur an extra charge? They seemed to be quite happy cashing cheques for all and sundry, but we who were account-holding business customers, the answer was "only at a cost." Where was the customer service? In this technological age, banks everywhere seem to be doing everything they can to deter individuals away from their premises, in favour of more and more web-based, international business — the kind that brings in mega-bucks. The bank manager would lean back in his expensive swivel chair, his eyes gleaming, as he pronounced:

"We have a policy in this bank, you know: you're expected to put some money *IN* occasionally!"

Huh.

Well now, things would be very different. And so it proved. When he realised the apparent size of our suddenly burgeoning financial assets, the bank manager was Mr. Charming himself.

Would we be interested in his brand new investment account?

No.

Would we be interested in a new off-shore account?

No.

Would he like to go and put his accounts where the sun doesn't shine?

That sorted, we instructed our solicitor to pay off the remainder of our mortgage and deduct his own quite modest charges and those of our estate agents. I couldn't understand why solicitors continue to charge such comparatively low rates compared with those of estate agents. But anyway, that's their business. We had our own affairs to consider.

Finally, after much heartache in disposing of all our unwanted belongings, we instructed a removals firm to move most of the remainder into a local storage depot. Him who shall be nameless of course couldn't resist asking whether, if the vehicle offloads our three-piece suite, the police will seek to re-cover it! And whether, if they advertise the accident as a 'shed load', whether people will start looking for a lot of sheds!

To keep costs down, we went along to supervise the loading of our stuff into the enormous metal cage that was allocated to us at the depot. The whole building resembled something from Colditz or, rather, Alcatraz. From within our individual 'cell', I stood with arms folded, staring out of the narrow window apertures, seeing nothing but a narrow strip of sunlight outside, a pale line of sky. For a moment I felt like a prisoner myself, seeing the dark shape of a bird flitting past the aperture outside. For a fleeting second I felt that I was the one in a cage, where bars held men prisoner, rather than the sweet birdsong of a pet canary. For weeks afterwards I had nightmares of being locked inside the cage, crammed up tight with all our belongings, not being able to escape. I wondered what a psychiatrist would make of that!

But this was my gateway to a better life. It was as if a dangling forty-watt flickering bulb, nearly engulfed by a cloud of life's fluttering chaotic images, was about to change from its yellow palsied state to a new chiaroscuro light.

Here was a heaven-sent opportunity beaming down from the heavens above, and I intended to take it.

4
A trip of a lifetime

Well, it's mid-January. You can tell by the fact the postman looks even more downcast than usual. Icy droplets are running from his cap down his beaky nose and into the top of his mail bag. His opinion of the weather and his overall feeling for life were pretty much evident:
"They say it does the gardens good. I couldn't care less."
Quite.
Yesterday I caught the corporation bus into the city centre. Whilst waiting at what remained of the graffiti-ridden state-of-the-art bus stop, I could hear the chimes of the nearby university clock striking the hour, preceded by its musical four chimes. It seemed to be ringing out the death knell of my working life — just a few more months to go.
Well good!
About time.
A stranger to the area asked me whether I knew the fare to the city centre. Unlike all other cities I could think of, strangers in this town are expected to know in advance the cost of the fare and the route of each bus. Illogical. The bus drew up. The driver as usual appeared surly, impatiently waiting with his engine idling, whilst I and the stranger fumbled with change. At last a long double white ticket issued forth from the machine and we both thankfully were able to walk down the aisle to a double orange and brown velour seat on the left. The driver seemed to take pleasure in crashing the gears of the old bus as we fell into the seat. It was clear that the driver's irritation at his poor job benefits was being transferred, with some schadenfreude, onto the poor unfortunate passengers. Thrown forwards, then

backwards, we all soon found ourselves becoming habitualised to the thrum of city traffic. I looked around at my fellow passengers. They all looked thoroughly immured to their daily grind, some nodding off to the throb of the engines. This was one of many city experiences I would soon gladly be leaving behind, including my innate depression.

As the bus crashed and groaned through the choked streets, my mind cast back to when H and I had first married, all those years ago. I was so young then, only nineteen, still in that adolescent, introverted stage. I had never even lived away from home, so was still a child really. I remembered that first house we had bought, managing to scrape together just sufficient to put down a small deposit.

It was in the early seventies, a time of national strikes and depression. I remembered the time vividly because I had been expecting our second child. Two candles had spluttered listlessly at the window, sporadically wavering as yet another winter gust found its way through the supposedly perfect patio doors, or so the pushy double glazing salesman had told me. The whole house lay dark and cold around us, as did the others in the Close. Only the ever-constant roar of the M5 motorway, fifty yards from our door, reminded me of the world outside, a world locked into the clamp-like vice of the burgeoning industrial strikes gripping the nation. First it had been the run on bread, then sugar, then the utility services depriving us of our basic needs. Tomorrow, or so our new T.V. announced, would bring more troubles as the refuse collectors threatened to join the strikers and even the burial services. Those in the Close young enough, like me, not to have lived through a world war mused that it must have been something like this thirty years ago. But it was the 1970s, for heaven's sake, not the depression years.

My misery had been compounded by our local newspaper trumpeting that many homes and businesses would be without electricity for up to nine hours a day, according to an announcement by the Central Electricity Generating Board. Miners were now into the sixth week of their strike over pay, had been picketing power stations and all other sources of fuel supply in an attempt to step up pressure on the Government. Electricity would be switched off on a rota basis between 0700 and 2400 every day. It said that consumers would face longer power cuts, up from six to nine hours. The shortage of electricity was forcing more and more factories and businesses to close. The Government had already imposed a three day week and a report in the Times newspaper claimed that over one million workers had now been laid off. Imperial Chemical Industries, one of the country's leading industries, had given a week's notice to all its sixty sixty-thousand weekly-paid staff as a precautionary measure. I had read that Government figures showed gas works were within a week of running out of power supplies. The miners had walked out on strike at the beginning of January in their first national dispute for fifty years. They were demanding a nine pounds a week pay rise on top of an average wage of twenty-five pounds The government offered a 7.9 per cent deal — just below its unofficial 8 per cent pay ceiling — but the National Union of Mineworkers refused to put it to the vote. The National Coal Board had then withdrawn the offer. The week previous to this a state of emergency had been declared. Two days later a committee of inquiry was established under Lord Wilberforce to investigate the miners' demands. All two hundred and eighty-nine pits in England and Wales were closed and the miners said they were prepared for a long fight.

I was so worried on the effect of all these deprivations on the coming child that I read everything I could lay my hands on in an attempt to work out a strategy for us all. I had known even back then that the area's population was awash with people and seemed to be increasing daily, the people moving to the city in their thousands to take up employment in its many industries. Whilst I had been growing up in the post-war years, a massive program of slum clearances had taken place, and vast city tracts were re-built, with overcrowded but strangely beautiful back-to-back housing being replaced by ugly high rise blocks of flats. I could understand the reasoning behind it, but knew even then that the planners had made a massive mistake that would be criticised by all and sundry for decades and even centuries to come.

Jerked back to the present by a lurching of the brakes, I shook my head clear of the past depressive years and hurried to alight from the bus before the swarm of eager passengers-to-be pushed me back up the stairs again.

Is it any wonder then that my depression had taken root? All my life I'd been a pessimist. At least, that's what everybody in England has been telling me for over fifty years, so it must be true, mustn't it? I was perplexed, therefore, to read in The Times that psychologists are at last coming round to the view that 'constructive negativism' can be quite a good thing. My family's origins derive from eastern Europe. Is this what I and many other people from eastern Europe have?

I vividly recall scenes from my childhood where my father, beset by the depression years, would lie flat on the floor staring vacantly up at the ceiling, arms behind his head, bemoaning his woes. So, I have been long familiar with what we deem to be pessimism. After all, aren't we regaled at length by such Jewish comics as Jackie Mason who prey on all our deepest misgivings ? It seems that those of us of *Ashkenazi* Russian descent are particularly prone to the syndrome, and now a genetic link has apparently been found. Of course, we all knew that really, deep down. There are so many of us who can recall our Russian/Polish grandmothers sitting with black scarves around their heads, despondent heads resting on a hand, giving that all pervasive and non-explanatory 'oi' at all the injustices in life.

What a surprise, then, to discover that eminent researchers in the U.S. have been studying the syndrome and have come up with some surprising conclusions. Not only have they discovered a genetic link but also that to have a constructive negativism mindset is a good thing after all. How can this be, I hear you say? We have long been conditioned, particularly by the Americans, to believe that optimism is everything. We must never be sad, depressed or despondent. We must instantly ignore the fact that there may have been a death in the family, for example, but jump up, smile, and get on with life.

Those of us who, like me, must really have constructive negativism know only too well how to use it to good effect. Research, apparently, has now proven that people with this newly-named syndrome actually do rather well in life. Optimists go through life happy and joyful, but are shocked when unforeseen things suddenly go wrong. They are often unable to work out what to do. Negativists, on the other hand, rely on the premise that at all times we need to work out what is the base-line (the worst that can possibly happen), and then formulate a strategy should it actually come to pass. They are usually the first to react when disasters happen in life (and they usually do, to all of us, at some time), because of course they have already foreseen it and worked out a plan. The crucial distinction here, then, is the difference between continual pessimism (which can affect your health, if taken to extremes, and can contribute to such tragedies as cancer) and the much-better constructive negativism.

Well, I'd been negative all my life in England but somehow had constructed something adventurous from everything that had happened to me. Now was the time to see whether a new life could somehow lift the oppressive veil that had hung, heavy and leaden, over my head for so long. No longer would I be melancholic and lost, surrounded by a world of chattering masses, drinking and enjoying themselves in the constant whirl that was everyday life. No longer would I sit in the corner of life's heady mysteries, head sunk in gloom like the absinthe drinker of Degas' fame, but would pull myself up, up and away to another world.

Time would tell.

Two days later and we are at last ensconced in our newly-rented furnished flat — a positive staging-post on our life's journey. The flat's quite nice really, as it needed to be to keep him happy. There are matching white sofas (yes, white – I wonder how long that will last) in the living room, and a very comfortable bed opposite glass sliding doors leading to a capacious wardrobe. I don't know if I can cope with that. minusculeWell, it's only for six months, after all.

No doubt fulfilling a deep subconscious need for the old and familiar, I wandered into the minuscule bathroom, where I began to take a mental inventory of the articles I had placed in the old medicine chest screwed haphazardly to the wall. (A few years later, I would be fascinated to discover a character in a William Styron novel doing something very similar). This ritual, almost autistic in its inexplicable, neurotic repetition, would soon become a pattern of mine whenever the outside world threatens to blot out the comforting though dull routines of everyday life. I suppose the feel of tactile, everyday essential commodities acts to restore some semblance of order in the chaos of life's changing pattern. Rather like running your hands up the long trunk of a tree, everything passes off as normal until, suddenly, a branch appears and you must choose which direction to take. Such was our life at the moment. Standing in front of the open wall cabinet of this unfamiliar bathroom, I was still able to run my fingers over the ordinary bathroom items I had placed within the night before. There on the shelves stood a can of Palmolive shaving mousse, the sort H had always liked, a box of Alka-Seltzer, a Gillette safety razor, two tubes of Colgate toothpaste, two Wisdom tooth brushes, one pink, one blue — rather like that old song by Max Bygraves, a bottle of expensive Canoe after-shave lotion, a bottle of Vosene anti-dandruff shampoo and Aquafresh shower gel, and a Boots silver-foil pack of aspirin. I touched them all gently, ostensibly re-arranging them so that the labels all faced to the front, before closing the door of the cabinet and returning to the settee in the living room. I suppose the whole episode only took about two minutes, but it seemed to reassure me nevertheless. Whatever happened in the future, I could still lay my hands on the reassuring presence of familiar things.

Tomorrow we set off on the journey that will decide our future. Every book we've ever read harps on about the fact that investing time and money in exploratory trips is rarely a waste. It will give us real knowledge about the place where we intend to live, warts and all, rather than relying on the airbrushed comments of others. Well, that's what the blurb says. But it shouldn't be too difficult, should it?

We decided to travel by Eurotunnel because of my congenital sea-sickness. It's more than sea-sickness, really — more like unilateral, comprehensive vertigo/comatositis. I well remember a previous journey across the Channel. How could I forget it? I ended up prostrate on the deck, where everyone who was everyone had told me was the best place to be. With all that health-giving, invigorating sea air, no-one could possibly be ill. One thing I learned. When you feel so ill that your whole body collapses, it's the loneliest place on earth. There is absolutely nothing you can do, nowhere you can go to escape the relentless swelling movement underneath. Somehow I still remember, lying dazed on the deck, how the other English travellers all managed carefully to step over my prostrate form, trying so hard to ignore this embarrassing person lying there in front of them. So, so English. Looking back though, the only crumb of comfort was the hazy memory of being picked up by a contingent of burly French sailors in orange jumpsuits and carted unceremoniously towards a vacant bunk cabin. Typical really. The only time I manage to obtain the complete attention of an impressive number of strong young French men, I am too weak to enjoy, or profit, from it. Although of little comfort, I later learned that that particular boat apparently had no stabilizers, so was especially rough. I wish I could get my hands on some form of strong medication. However, it doesn't seem to matter how many tablets or even injections I take, they haven't invented anything yet that even approaches what I need when travelling by sea.

There are some people who tell me that my affliction is all psychological and that I should pull myself together. They say it's just fear really. Well, I tell them that no, it's certainly not fear. I can at least swim a little. Whereas no matter how hard I try, I can't fly! If it were psychological, I would suffer far more actual sickness in a plane and that doesn't appear to be the case because travel tablets eradicate it. Don't get me wrong; I still hate flying, but it's not because of travel sickness: it's the fact that I don't like falling out of the sky. I can never understand why planes aren't equipped with parachutes instead of life-jackets. I mean, so many things can go wrong. The pilot might be drunk or ill. The mechanic who repaired the faulty nuts on the wings and engines might have been tired, etc. etc. Why should everything on the plane be absolutely hunky-dory just when I decide to fly? It stands to reason that, sod's law being what it is, something's going to go wrong sometime I'm on board. I know what you're thinking. There are far more deaths on the roads and that flying is the safest form of transport. That may well be. But there are far more variables on the roads. If the engine fails or a tyre blows, we can just stop and steer into the emergency lane. And if someone actually slams into us, there is the chance we will end up injured and transported to hospital. What I mean is: there are innumerable chances of living to travel another day, but in a plane? Forget it.

Anyway, today we plan to go via Eurotunnel. Everything should be just fine. There are no boats, just a train to transport us under the Channel. Now then, where's that route map? Ah yes, as usual, stained, crumpled and split underneath the back seat of the car. Why is it that whenever you need to find a map co-ordinate, it's always obliterated by the crease or central spine of the map?

Jobsworth

The journey down to Folkestone, despite my misgivings, proved to be surprisingly easy. The M20 was as busy as usual, but we found junction 11A without a lengthy delay and drove straight to the check-in booth. However, we soon found that for some peculiar reason you are not allowed to check in more than two hours before the journey. This seemed completely at odds with airport rules, but what do I know? We therefore had to kick our heels and tootle around the delights of Folkestone town centre for a couple of hours before retracing our steps back to the check-in. This time all was fine, and the officious person allowed us in. A song penned by an Australian, heard on local radio, came to mind:

Jobsworth, jobsworth
It's more than my job's worth
I don't care, rain or snow
Whatever you want
The answer's No!

I can keep you standing
Forever in the queue
And if you don't like it
You know what you can do!
John Williams

Doesn't that just sum up the attitude of so many jumped-up petty English officials. Well, that's one thing we hope to bypass very soon.

The half an hour rule, to allow for security checks at the British frontier control, seemed to us to be completely reasonable, however. All we needed to find was our booking reference number and the debit card number we used to make our booking. I searched through the enormous cavernous container that passes as my handbag these days. Well, I need to have somewhere to put all those things that him indoors wouldn't possibly think of in advance. I don't know what he would do without me. It was then I remembered that I had booked our passage on-line whilst at work. The official repeated that I needed to show the long number that appeared on the booking confirmation screen when I booked it.

Help!

Eventually, the official suggested we may prefer to take our time and use the simple self check-in point. She said this was easy enough for a child to handle and would allow us to check in in our own time. Yeah, right. We drove over, following the signs to the kiosks located before the main

43

booths and attempted to follow the foolproof step-by-step instructions displayed on the touch screens. Eventually, miraculously, I found that elusive long registration number I needed. It was hiding at the bottom of my bag, under last year's squashed lipstick, which had jammed an old hairgrip into the creases. Eventually, amazingly, we managed to print out our very own departure hanger, and hooked it behind the wing mirror as instructed.

Hugh sighs of relief.

In no time at all we had eaten a light (Mazda!) lunch, after paying through the nose at the refreshment stop, and driven straight through the frontier controls. We expected passport control to be difficult, as the faces on our British passports made him indoors look like convict 99, and me like his grandmother. The trouble with passport photos is that you are forever reminded of that collar that wouldn't lie straight or that glaring, embarrassing carbuncle on your nose that appeared on the day of the photo. Over the years we got used to the suppressed smirks of amusement at passport controls around the world. But what the hell.

Signs pertinently asked us to ensure that we had a warning triangle, headlight converters, GB sticker, spare bulb kit, fire extinguisher, first aid kit and reflective fluorescent vest in the boot.

"Will my green vest do — you know, the one that changed colour in the wash?" he asked me innocently.

"Hmm."

Apparently all the leading organisations and ferry companies give out similar information about what equipment drivers legally need to have in their cars in France. Under the heading "Motoring in Europe – are you legal?" their leaflets all list triangles, spare bulbs, first aid kits and fire extinguishers without stating that, in fact, none are actually legal requirements at all for France. All the leaflets, naturally, give maps of their shop where you can purchase all these items. Of course, it's all a scam so that they can cream off up to sixty pounds sterling from all us gullible travellers. A policeman later told me that according to the French government no less, the only legal requirements are adaptors on headlights and a GB plate on the rear of the car. Enough said.

Just as well then! And had we adjusted our headlights to drive on the right? Well, we wouldn't be driving at night, would we, so that shouldn't be necessary, should it?

The journey itself proved to be amazingly swift, once we had manoeuvred our vehicle through the bumpy rail ramps onto the train. Him indoors could even get out and stretch his legs during the journey. But for me, it was important to hold on tight in case of emergency. Each time the overhead visual display rolled its announcements, I jumped in case this was the time that we had to flee. But everything seemed fine. I even got used to the appalling French accent of the train announcer. My French isn't perfect, but I was sure that the word Euros shouldn't be pronounced like Yoorowes complete with Tyneside accent!

At last, we were in France and hurtling south at an amazing rate. We soon found, though, that the French road rules were somewhat different than in the U.K. After a few near-miss encounters that had me reaching for the Valium, we learned that priority must always be given to the car coming from the right-hand side, and that those funny yellow lozenge signposts at the side of the road actually show that main road traffic has priority over traffic joining from a side-road on the right. Him indoors who does the driving said I should have known that.

We had found the rue Chevreul, though, without even trying and were soon heading down the A16, even though the signs worryingly pointed to Calais Port Car Ferry. *No. Surely we can't be heading back where we came from?* But no, we seemed to be O.K. and were soon zooming through the entrance to the A26 towards Paris.

"See? Easy. Easy," I gloated.

Always a portent of doom.

On the main autoroute we discovered that those huge signs every few kilometres proclaiming 'Aire de' this and 'Aire de' that were actually service stations where you could stop and use the facilities. Hugh sighs of relief from him doing the driving. Trouble was that at too many of these wayside stops, women were expected to use a hole in the ground. Me? At my age? If I tried to squat, I'd never get up again. No thank you. So I crossed my legs and waited for somewhere more convenient, in every sense of the word. After a while I realised that if the sign for the 'Aire de.' displayed a knife and fork, then the facilities would be modern. Oh well. There's nothing like trial and error in this great new adventure of ours.

Another thing we discovered was that a good sense of timing was essential in France. The French eat at very set times and if you miss these proscribed times, you go hungry. For breakfast, don't have a huge English fry-up because then you won't be ready to eat at 12 noon. Disaster! What you must do is take coffee and a croissant at 8 a.m. and then nothing else until noon. Then voilà! You are ready for lunch at the proscribed hour. Most foreign travellers find to their cost that if you miss the 12 – 2 p.m. lunch hour slot, most rural restaurants are then closed until 7.30 p.m. when they open again for dinner.

Disaster narrowly averted

We had arranged to take an overnight stop in Orléans, rather than Paris. We reckoned it should be cheaper there and not so difficult to circumnavigate. Unfortunately, my navigating en route left much to be desired, not helped by the fact it was now pitch black outside and a heavy rain was pelting against the windscreen. Despite the fact the wipers were racing back and forth like the clappers, visibility was almost nil as we hit the Paris périphérique.

"I thought the whole idea was to avoid Paris?" innocently from him doing the driving.

I peered squinting at the creased route map, brows furrowed in concentration.

"I know! I know! I can't understand it."

I looked helplessly all around. French lorries loomed menacingly, nose to tail, limp Gauloises hanging from lower lips in Gallic disgust at 'les rosbifs' who had the temerity to transgress their routes. You could just hear them thinking: *merde! If they don't even know where they're going, why don't they stay in their own country where they belong?*

"Well, come on. I need to know which road to take. Hurry up, woman!"

"Oh God. I suppose you'd better go right."

We swung heavily to the right, at the very last minute, before one of those ubiquitous green and white arrow signs that sit either side of important exit roads. Unlike the U.K. where exit signs are highlighted miles ahead of time, in France they appear right in front of the exit. Not good for the blood pressure. We soon found ourselves on a narrow road seemingly going nowhere.

"Look. There's a roundabout ahead." Hopefully.

"Which way then?" resignedly.

"Try right."

I suppose we knew we had done something catastrophically wrong by the loud horns from passing French lorries. Certainly the bumpy terrain should have informed us immediately that all was not right.

"Oh my God," said him at the wheel, not known for his extreme mood swings. "We're on a rail track!!"

"Oh my God," in synchrony. "Quick. Back up. Back up!" Panic-stricken.

"I'm trying to!"

"At least, it isn't Paris. I mean, then we might have been in-sane…"

The road to hell

Looking back later on this incident, we could only breathe a sigh of relief that the hourly train at this juncture had not yet been due. That's eight of our nine lives gone then. Fortunately, we miraculously soon found ourselves back on track – well, not exactly back on track — but on the A26 approaching a toll booth. I searched frantically in the section of my capacious purse for my French coins.

"How much do I need?"

"How do I know?"

We pulled up in front of those enormous twenty-lane booths, trying to figure out what those blue strange box symbols were which highlighted most of the lanes. In the end we chose one with a green arrow, only to find that we didn't need money yet. It was just to get a ticket. I shoved it in the special pocket behind the sun visor as we narrowly avoided hitting the perilously narrow exit barrier.

"That's good," said I foolishly. "We didn't have to pay anything."

"In this life," said he laconically, "just wait a while, and a paying opportunity will surely avail itself." There spoke the man of business doom and gloom — a man of many years' experience in such matters.

And so it proved, when yet another enormous toll booth alleyway hit us full on. This time it cost us 19.20 euros. I spluttered "why, that must be at least a tenner…"

"Told you…" smugly.

We later learned that the annoying cars that seemed to speed through these tolls without paying anything in fact had a *télépéage* box fitted in their car. This allowed them to sail through the *péage* lanes marked with a 'T', whilst the rest of we ordinary mortals fumed in the heat.

Still smarting about the money we'd spent, the rest of the journey progressed smoothly enough. Well, for us anyway. Soon, thankfully, we had pulled off the autoroute and tooled into our three-star hotel in Orléans.

"Do you know why it's called three star?"

"You can see them through the hole in the roof."

Aargh.

Why do so many French budget hotels not have restaurants on the premises? You'd think in the land of *bien manger* that would be la pièce de la résistance, but no. All too often they serve breakfast *prêt à porter*, that's breakfast French-style – rolls and coffee — but for dinner you have to go out and about. And all we could find nearby was an American theme restaurant. Well, that certainly suited our very own long-distance driver, so he got stuck in whilst I had to forgo yet again my sporadic diet.

The following day, fresh from a night's tossing, turning and blanket tugging — why can't the French make beds big enough — we were on our way again, dragging our tails behind us. To while away the long hours at the wheel, my other half decided to play one of his favourite CDs. However, I couldn't help wondering at his choice when I heard the dulcet tones of Van Morrison singing laconically that we were on the road to hell.

Soon we'd seamlessly bypassed the Quai de la Madeleine, Saint Jean de la Ruelle and La Chapelle Saint Mesmin before zooming along on the A71 followed by the endless A20 to all points south. Thinking back to our near-accident, I breathed a sigh of relief that we hadn't gathered any points on our licence. I was slightly concerned, though, that our new international licences still had our old UK address printed on them. I had read that, once we are permanently resident in France, should we incur any driving penalties, we would need to get a new French licence. The DVLA apparently does not permit the renewal of UK licences with foreign address.

Himself said that he'd read that in France drivers with clean licences have taken to selling their details via the internet for fees of over two thousand euros in return for taking other people's penalty points. He said that French drivers apparently start with twelve points and lose them for offences. Some drivers were now selling the use of their details on the speeding forms so the driver can claim they were not driving at the time of the offence. The seller (not the driver) then loses points. Although in theory giving a wrong name could attract a fine of over one thousand euros and even a jail sentence, the French police admit they do not have sufficient time to check out such scams.

"What's the difference between the French police and the gendarmes?" I asked innocently.

"You've heard of Jean d'arc?"

"Yeees?" apprehensively.

"Well, because they've all got long arms, they're called Jean d'arms...."

"Oh God. There's no escape."

We motored on, thankfully in silence. Despite being in the depths of one of the coldest months of the year in England, here the sky was blue and the air clean and health-giving. Ah, this was the life. We felt invigorated for the first time for months and ready for our new challenge.

After all, whatever could go wrong?

5
Gendarmes, Landladies and Weary Travellers

We've finally arrived, a little travel weary and hot, but definitely still alive and kicking. The car door creaked and squealed on its hinges as I flung it wide, only to have it bang on my sore knee a second later. Why does it always do that?

"Did you say something, dear?"

"Does my voice normally sound like it needs oiling, or something?" sarcastically.

The local agent had booked us into a B&B whilst we searched for our dream house so now all that was required was to find the B&B. Shouldn't be too difficult, we thought, as this was only a very tiny place, but search as we may, could we find it? Eventually I spotted a gendarmerie at the edge of the village, so bravely entered its darkened portals and tried out my French.

"Excusez-moi, Monsieur, mais nous cherchons La Créperie."

"Bouff. Tous les restaurants sont fermés en hiver, Madame."

"Non, non. La Créperie est un B et B…"

The officer scratched his nose awhile, asked an invisible colleague apparently ensconced further inside in the gloom, then emerged triumphant.

"Oui, Madame. Suivre la voiture."

I raced out to our car.

"I think he said we were to follow him."

We hastily turned the ignition and followed the policeman, trying not to breathe in the diesel fumes and narrowly avoiding the swirl of gravel in his wake as he did a hand-brake turn. He led us through innumerable tiny alleyways, so minuscule that we thought the car couldn't possibly fit, but we had no choice. It was either follow that car, or continue lost and earn the wrath of the local gendarmerie. This was not how we wanted to start our new life here so we followed the car, until with a flourish and a loud voilà, we saw the unmistakeable sign:

La Créperie

Him of the laconic bent opined whilst glancing up at the façade: "Now I see why they call it that."

"Shh." Honestly, you can't take him anywhere a second time without apologising for the first. We thanked the policeman and, laden with our luggage, entered at last our haven for the next week or so whilst we house-hunted.

Madame was all smiles as she welcomed us and bade us follow her up the steep, rickety wooden steps to the second floor. I have always thought that landladies benefit from letting rooms at the top of the house by the fact that tenants are always so weary after climbing all those innumerable stairs with luggage in tow that they invariably collapse in a thankful heap on the bed, rather than look around and complain. And so it proved. Still, tomorrow was the day — the day we started our house hunting in earnest.

Even he couldn't wait.

6
Searching for that dream French house

The English estate agency was situated on a quaint cobbled street in a picturesque part of the village. Opposite was the ancient *Place de la Halle*, which from mediaeval times had housed the weekly market. Today, not being the market day, it was filled with school children running and shouting through the pillars and oriols. We stared down the cobbled alleyway in amazement. It really was a wondrous sight. Everywhere were many-storied ancient houses, each one a photographer's dream, their many windows edged with the colourful cornflower-blue *volets* of the region. We peered into the window of a private art gallery and were spellbound by the pot pourri of artists' easels. Everywhere were examples of vivid impressionist landscapes, with their bright splotches and melange of shades, flowers and cornfields. In one corner there was one painting reminding us of a famous Pissarro. With one broad brushstroke it successfully depicted a hushed Sunday afternoon, all verdant vines, crumbling sun-baked masonry and a vision of the future catching the last fading glow of summer's elusive light.

We walked back to the agency's window and glanced at the colourful postcards pinned in the window. So many glorious stone houses were for sale, complete with swimming pools, all pictured under navy blue skies. Ah yes; this was what we wanted. We pushed open the door and walked confidently in.

"We have an appointment at 10 a.m."

The phone jangled. "Excuse me a moment." The moment lasted twenty minutes.

Why is it that staff always jump to answer the phone, at

the expense of the people who have made the effort to appear in person. Just calm down, calm down and relax.

We walked over to look at some enlarged photos of some very impressive houses in the region. Unfortunately, on putting on our reading glasses, the small-print prices also looked very impressive. Way beyond our agreed budget.

He whispered, "I thought you said houses in this region were supposed to be cheap."

"Shh, she's coming back."

She brushed a tendril of hair off her perspiring forehead and apologised for the delay. "Sorry about that. It gets pretty hectic in here, as you can see." She waved her hand airily around the office, where a harassed assistant was also answering phones ten to the dozen. "Now then, what exactly is your budget range?" She obviously liked getting straight away down to the nitty-gritty.

"Well, actually, we were rather hoping to find something in the hundred to two hundred thousand euros mark…"

"Oh," followed by a short intake of breath, as she sat down at her desk and began rummaging in the stacks of folders lying haphazardly on her old wooden desk. "Well, we do have a range here somewhere. Let me see…..Ah yes, here it is. What I suggest is that you take this folder and go through it slowly over there…," pointing to a desk in a dark corner away from the more prestigious house photos we saw earlier.

Obediently, we did as we were told, skulking with some embarrassment over to the obviously lower-priced area of the office. We sat down heavily as the agent's phone began jangling incessantly once again. We could hear her voice, suddenly transformed "Bonjour Monsieur Feret. Ça va? Ah, vous avez choisi la maison grande à huit cents milles? Bon, très bon!"

I could hear my other half's teeth gnashing in snarling frustration.

"Don't worry," I whispered back. "I'm sure we'll find something in here to suit us," glancing hopefully at the folder in front of us. "I mean they must want to sell these or they wouldn't have included them in their repertoire, would they?"

I could see a glazed look come into his eyes. We had less than a fortnight to find our house or we were heading for homelessness. The clock on our flat rental back home was counting down, and then we would be out on the streets. No. I was determined that it wouldn't come to that. Surely one of these houses would suit us?

The agent put down the phone, stood up and hurried over to us.

"Well, how are you two getting on? Found anything you like?"

I pointed out all the ones that were hovering around the one fify thousand mark, or rather one fifty-thousand euros. She smiled and said, "Good. I'll just get the car and we'll go and take a look."

We were flummoxed. We hadn't realised that she herself would take us round every one of them right this minute. I hid my surprise, gathered my large bag and creaking husband and followed her smartly out of the shop and over the greasy cobbles to her car.

Overhead a few drops of fine rain had just started to fall, making our way slippery.

"Probably the only rain all day," grumbled him indoors.

"Stop being like Victor Meldrew," I hissed, as we rushed after her disappearing figure as she sharply turned a corner into another tiny alleyway. Looking up, it seemed as though the residents on either side could shake hands with each other, if they had a mind, so close were their leaning turret windows. Amazing.

"Here we are," she called, as we carefully picked our way after her, trying to avoid the dog mess everywhere.

"Damn, too late," said he, struggling to scrape his shoes on the crépi walls either side.

"Don't do that!" *Oh God, why are husbands like children sometimes?*

And so began the journey from hell. The agent drove like a lunatic around the winding country roads, obviously keen to keep to her tight time schedule, with me feeling the onset of my usual nausea. I took several deep breaths and opened a window, only to let in a gust of cold, misty air making everyone inside cough. I closed it again and suffered in silence.

"Ah, here we are," the agent said brightly.

We looked out. Was this the first property that looked so impressive in the photo? What had seemed like a property with lots of space turned out to be jammed in the middle of a courtyard. We knew as soon as we saw it that it wasn't for us, but we dutifully walked around it. She soon saw, though, from our unspoken body language that it was time to move on to property two. This had plenty of space but was so ramshackle that it would take thousands of pounds of renovation to bring up to standard. Our faces fell and we started to panic. And so the property tour continued, from one disaster after another, with the best one unfortunately having a stone tomb in the grounds at the front, complete with large cross and rosary beads to the fore. We couldn't live, looking out at that every morning.

Eventually, after hours of looking, we returned dejectedly to the agency.

"I don't know what we're going to do," I confided to the agent. "We simply must find something on this trip, or we'll be homeless."

She looked thoughtful for a moment, before coming up with an idea. "I think you'd do better with a more modern property than the ones we sell. Would you like me to introduce you to a colleague who runs an agency round the corner? They have some modern properties that I'm sure would suit you better?"

"Oh, are you sure?" foolishly. "I mean, aren't they your competition?"

She laughed. "This is France, my dear. We have lots of arrangements like this, where the welcoming agency pays a commission to the introducing agent when a sale is forthcoming." She smiled.

"Oh, I see," I replied. "Well, yes, of course we'd like to

see what your colleague has to offer."

The agent was quickly on the phone, speaking in rapid French, but with an unmistakeable English accent, making it quite easy to follow. She put down the phone, explaining that the other agency was owned and run by a Dutch couple who were pretty much tri-lingual. She ushered us to the door and pointed down the cobbled street to an orange sign we could just make out in the distance. Wasn't orange the Dutch football team colour? queried H. *Not now, H, not now*. The agent closed the door with a flourish, no doubt happy to be rid of us. We walked away, each of us strangely silent as we contemplated what would happen if this also proved a disaster.

The fog which had been hanging over us like a blanket all morning now seemed to be rising, lifting my spirits a little as we wended our way towards the orange sign beckoning to us at the end of the street. We glanced at the large picture window and immediately spotted the photo of a rather pretty bungalow with blue shutters.

"How much?" from him.

I peered a little closer. "Actually, it's in our price range." Hope springs eternal. We climbed up the steep stone step and pushed open the stiff door. A loud bell clanged in the distance.

"Enough to wake the dead."

"Shh."

A tall, smiling man came forward to welcome us. I knew instinctively that this must be the Dutch owner. For one thing, all Frenchmen seemed to be short and this man looked well over six feet.

"Hello," in impeccable English. Yes, he must be Dutch. What is it about all the Dutch and the Germans that even the roadsweepers can argue about the politics of the day or on every subject under the sun in perfect English, whilst we English……

"We rather like the look of that bungalow in the window. Could we take a look at it?"

He looked at his watch. It was five to twelve, the

inviolable French lunchtime, when everything that moves closes for lunch. "I tell you what. We're just about to close for lunch, but I've got a leaflet on the property here. Why don't we meet up at two, right after lunch, which will give you time to consider it in more detail?"

We agreed that was a good idea and shook hands.

"Bon appetit."

"A bientôt," we chorused, suddenly cheerful at this new turn of events.

You won't believe this, but the leaflet he gave us was in Dutch! I think he must have run out of English versions, but that didn't help us much. I searched my memory-banks for snippets of German learned a long time ago to try to make sense of the thing.

"*De woning is goed onderhouden en is gelegen op een perceel van 2133 m^2 aan de rand van een middeleeuws dorp.*"

"Huh? I'm going straight back to tell him what I think of him. Does he want to sell this place or not? How anyone is supposed to understand such double-Dutch I don't know!"

"Look. Don't panic," optimistically from me. "I think *woning* means habitation and *perceel van 2133 m^2* means the number is the land size. That looks good. And in any case, I'll know straight away if it's the place for us when we see it. I have a gut instinct for this one. Just trust me…"

"Hmm."

At two-fifteen the pleasant Dutchman returned. We were already learning. Nothing moves fast in France, and especially not after the all-important midday meal.

"You have eaten well?"

We nodded, not wishing to tell him that after we had eliminated the escargots, the cassoulet (didn't know what was in it) and other strange concoctions on the lunch-time menu of the local bar, we had dined on a simple pizza.

"O.K. then. Follow me," a black shiny folder underneath his arm.

We followed him out of the agency, with me nearly falling

down the steep step onto the cobbles below. Just saved myself from this undignified ignominy in the nick of time.

The fine drizzle and fog of earlier had now given way to a wondrous blue sky with not a cloud in sight. This was more like it. We raced after the agent, our creaking knees no match for his long, lengthy strides until, disappearing suddenly around another one of those sharp corners, we found ourselves in the main Place de la Halle. He marched over to his Renault 5 and our hearts sunk. Were we all to fit into this tiny vehicle? The agent saw our faces and laughed heartily. "Don't worry. There's room enough for us all."

"Yeah. Right."

There were only three doors, so he opened the passenger side and we struggled into the back, bent double with the effort before collapsing onto the back seat. He clanged the door shut several times before it engaged, then walked around and jumped into the driver's seat, somehow expertly folding his long legs into the cramped space inside.

"This is cozy, isn't it?"

Silence from the back.

He cranked the car into some form of spluttering life and we were off, skidding around the greasy cobbled alleyways until thankfully onto a tarmac road. He raced along at breakneck speed. I couldn't see the speedometer but felt sure that the speed limits around here weren't meant to accommodate Stirling Moss. Still, we tried to relax and couldn't help but admire the wondrous scenery flashing past. This was more like it. Somewhat different from High Street back home. I had a sudden thought: "Oh God. We don't actually have a home right now." I suppressed it and stared dazedly out of the window again. Everything seemed so surreal somehow, as if in a dream. I shook my head to clear my thoughts. This was important. I must make the right decision, a decision that would affect the rest of our lives.

"Oh God."

Eventually I spotted the name of the village on the Dutch leaflet: Paradis de Quercy, heralded by a red and white sign, with another language printed beneath. Yes, this must be the village, but what did the sign mean? The agent laughed and explained that all signs in the region had the old Occitan name printed underneath. It was a way of preserving the heritage of the region. He cranked up the brake handle before fully stopping the car, throwing us all forward momentarily, whilst he studied the property address again. Then suddenly we were off again, careering around corners and doing handbrake turns before finally, with a triumphant 'Voilà!', we were turning into a long shingle driveway. We had arrived.

I scrambled out and gazed up at the house, which was positioned on a rise, slightly to the right of the long, curving driveway. "Look," I said to my other half. "It's got crépi walls."

"I think it looks rather nice."

Exasperation.

We both stood and stared again at the house. I knew instinctively, just as I knew I would, that this was our house. It looked positively beautiful with its Mediterranean blue shutters, rose bushes around the door, and long stone terrace in the front. All around us were numerous variegated trees and shrubs, including plum, oak, balsam poplar and chestnut, interspersed with rolling green grass.

In the doorway emerged Monsieur and Madame, the owners, come to greet these strange English people. We all shook hands and said Bonjour, before Madame ushered us inside. My mind momentarily cast back to all the other French houses we had viewed so far, and the dark, crumbling inner décor we had discovered. I held my breath. Inside, I knew at once that this was for us. It had a beautiful natural stone fireplace, complete with *insert*, which Monsieur explained was a log-burning stove. Set above the *insert* was a heavy dark oak mantelpiece, the sort that everyone craves but rarely finds in England. We walked into the kitchen. Having already made my mind up, I dismissed the lack of facilities, knowing that him indoors would soon arrange something more suited to our English tastes. We completed the tour, noting the house was surprisingly spacious for a bungalow, with its three bedrooms and bathroom.

Monsieur was evidently pleased with the sunken bath. He beckoned to him who knows. "Regardez," he pointed. I could tell from the response that my other half was already picturing stumbling into that great hole and not being able to get out again. At least he didn't say he'd look into it. Clearly, the sunken bath would have to go. Pity really. I rather fancied wallowing in Roman splendour, cavorting amongst the billowing soap suds of my subterranean pleasure retreat. Oh well.

Glancing in the mirror above the washbasin reminded me of how, as tall Europeans, we always seem to get caught out by short plumbers. It always seems to be the plumber who fixes the height of the mirror. He will always adjust it according to whether he can see his own face reflected back, forgetting that for ever more the taller owners of the mirror will suffer hernias from constantly crouching to see themselves in it! Why are plumbers always short anyway? And you should always beware of shaking hands with a plumber, or even a gynaecologist, because you never know where they've been!

We all walked out through the kitchen door into the back. The view was spectacular. "Regardez," repeated Monsieur, evidently sure that this would be the only French word we were likely to understand. The view certainly was wonderful and a million miles away from the tightly-packed, graffiti-ridden English suburban views back home. We could see for miles, the view permeated here and there by densely-wooded copses, undulating steadily into the distance. Without actually expressing it, I had been searching all my life for complete privacy such as this, and now we seemed to have found it.

Him whose mind always turns to money took Monsieur to one side. "C'est combien?" Wonderful how his French improves when the need arises.

"Un cent et quarante-neuf milles euros."

"Uh. You take one hundred and forty…?" hopefully.

"Non!" hands facing downwards, one moving forcefully over the other in the international sign language indicating disapproval.

We had often talked about the usually unknown reasons why people sell, so we asked the vendor our standard three questions: "Why are you selling, why are you selling, why are you selling?"

To which came the carefully prepared response: "The land is now too large for us." (This all sounded eminently sensible, but we later discovered the vendor had bought a new plot of land in the village, double the size of this one!) This all goes to prove that when buying an established house, one never knows the real reason for the sale.

After a further few minutes of kicking our heels in frustration, the agent walked up to us, confirming that the owner definitely would not accept anything less than the asking price. What did we want to do?

There was no question that this was the only house we had seen that had even come close to 'ticking all the boxes.'" It was habitable without doing major structural repairs, had privacy, space for him indoors to crash and bang to his heart's content, was within walking distance of the village with its Boulangerie (I could smell those warm croissants now), and was within our budget.

We shook hands all around.

It seemed that we had bought our dream house.

Let the future begin!

Reports and notaires

One stroke of good fortune was discovering that the B & B landlady's husband was a civil engineer. The agent told us that French people don't usually bother with a survey before purchasing a property, merely doing structural work as and when needed. However, we had been conditioned to seek some sort of survey so were pleased to find an English professional to give our property the once-over before the end of the seven day cooling off period which purchasers are given in France before signing the *compromis de vente* or to retract after having signed the deed.

"Just as well we found the house in our first week then," responded him indoors to this news. And, of course, he was right. It meant that we could await the engineer's report and, if all was well, sign the agreement before leaving France. We discovered that house purchase solicitors in France are called notaires, and unlike in England, are disinterested parties to the transaction, i.e., they act for neither the vendor nor the buyer. They seem to act solely for the government, as far as I could see. We learned that the seven day cooling off period runs from the date on which the notaire notifies the potential purchaser of the completed draft deed of sale or gives him a copy in return for a signed receipt. Apparently the deed of sale may not be signed before the expiration of this period.

We needed also to ensure that our *compromis* agreement contained the following provisions:

- identification of the property being sold (well yes!);
- a guarantee of the absence of asbestos;
- certificates regarding elimination of termites, lead etc.;
- the terms of the purchase;
- the price and date of payments ('hah hah,' from you know who);
- the date for taking possession.

During that final seven days in France we waited with bated breath for the engineer's report. It was hardly life or death, but it felt that way. Dependent on what he found would be our whole future. We weren't so much buying a house; the house was the catalyst which would give us a new future. Two days before the end of the seven days the engineer arrived with his ten page report. My eyes, long trained to skim-read and summarise wordy university documents, flipped frantically to his final conclusion:

Overall opinion...

"He wasn't wearing an overall," from him indoors.
"Shh, I'm trying to read."

The property offers good, spacious and airy accommodation with good-sized rooms and has a gas central heating system. I found no evidence of any significant defects or shortcomings other than those mentioned in Section F.....

"F's a good letter to use for telling us we've been stuffed......" says he. I've given up on his laconic sense of humour after nearly forty years of suffering, so I blithely continued reading.

Readily occupiable upon vacant possession.

By now we both fearfully flipped to that ominous *Section F*, labelled *Action:*

Dampness in external render needs to be addressed...

Chimneys should be swept and the steel flue liner and access point to the flush fitted insert burner should be checked with the owner.

Need to discover how storm water is disposed of — could not be seen on inspection.

It should be established by the notaire where the responsibilities lie with regard to water escaping from someone else's property and what the insurance position is.

With some relief I turned to the engineer.
"So, what does all this mean? Are you saying that in your professional opinion we're O.K. to sign the *compromis de vente*?"
"Yes. The points I made under Section F are the normal types of action that purchasers should expect to carry out when buying an older property, but are nothing unusual. I therefore see no reason why you can't sign the *compromis* and go ahead with your purchase."
Hallelujah.

And so we went ahead. The process of buying and selling houses is so different in France, and on reflection I much prefer the French way of doing it. Every time the purchaser needs to sign anything at the notaire's office, the vendors and the participating estate agents all attend and discuss the situation in the one office. The *compromis* agreement even included a statement testifying to the absence of such things as termites or asbestos, lead , etc. These are all things I probably wouldn't have thought to ask in the heat of the moment. Whereas in England….everything seems to be handled over the phone and by post, sometimes not meeting the solicitor in person throughout the whole transaction.

Another thing I'm surprised about is that we need to add a special clause to the final sale agreement, effectively altering French final testament laws in leaving the property to a spouse instead of to any surviving children. You live and learn. What was also a particularly nasty shock was the size of the notaire's fees. At eight percent, this was considerably higher than the one percent charged in England.

"At least the agent's fees were already included in the selling price," said he, "so we didn't need to pay anything to them."

"I suppose so." I grabbed the calculator to work out whether we would shortly be in hock to all and sundry to pay for it all.

Well, tomorrow we return to England. Everything's been done and signed for. We've arranged to sign the final paperwork and pay the final ninety percent when we return in May. Pleased, smug smile of satisfaction. May is the end of the six-month flat rental period in England.

"Have I been clever or what?" to no-one in particular.

"No, just smug as usual."

Pillow throwing time.

7
Back to England

Icy rain's pelting against the windows of my office, letting me know in no uncertain terms that I am back in the land of too many people, too many cars and not enough space. As I stare at the rain-sodden skies, my mind keeps returning to those final days in paradise, or *Paradis* I should say. What a stroke of luck to find that house when we did. I really don't know what we'd have done if we hadn't found it during that nervous fourteen days search.

My eyes glance up at the clock on the wall, fixed high up above the empty wall-planner that someone pinned up last Christmas.

08.45.

I never used to be this early; must be all the excitement. I take the opportunity to switch on my PC and check if our French agent has sent me that email attachment he promised.

Yes! I love email. I click on the attachment and, voilà, there's our new house taking up the whole of the screen in all its glory. Two colleagues slowly drift in, dragging dripping umbrellas in their wake. They brighten up momentarily on seeing me.

"You're back then," rhetorically.

"Certainly looks like it," I counter, grinning broadly.

A third arrives, glancing at the clock to see if her lateness has been observed.

"You're back then."

"Yes."

Three pairs of eyes gleam as, shorn of their sodden outer garments and making their way to the kettle in the corner, they await my news.

"Well?" they chorus. "What happened in France?"

I smiled, savouring the moment.

"Well, I did it!"

"No," all ears flapping.

"Yeah. We've bought a house and paid the deposit."

"Oh my God," they responded. "That means you really will be leaving us, then," said the nearest, glancing at her other colleagues.

Probably calculating between themselves on their own chances of promotion once I've left! I thought, but kept it to myself. Better left unsaid.

"Yes. We thought we'd probably make the big move in May, by which time all the paperwork should be ready to sign and complete the deal."

"Wow!"

"I know. That's what I thought. Can't really believe it."

"So, when do you think you'll be handing in your notice?"

The others looked momentarily taken aback at the directness of the question, but I didn't mind. I had foreseen all of this.

"Oh, in due course, as soon as I've given some thought to the wording. Something as important as that, after nearly thirty years of working here, shouldn't be rushed, don't you think."

I leaned back in my chair, the arms as usual creaking their disapproval as they always had.

The girls, after a moment or two to digest all of this amazing information, then asked:

"So, what's it like?"

"What?" innocently.

"The house, silly. I bet it's really romantic and French."

"You've got to understand that we were on a strict budget so don't expect to see a chateau or anything."

"You mean you've got a picture to show us?" crowding around my console.

"Wow."

As the days wore on, the news slowly leaked out, like the

proverbial grapevine. Even our laconic storesman, who worked down in the basement, couldn't help but mutter:

"You lucky, lucky lady."

"No. You don't understand," I told him. "I haven't won the lottery, you know. Anyone can do what I've done. All you need are the three essential ingredients:

An occupational pension that can be claimed now – however small;
A U.K. house that is paid for or with just a small mortgage left;
No interfering relatives or dependents to put a spoke in the wheel."

The academics around the place were as sceptical as the storesman.

"Oh," they all blithely opined. "I couldn't possibly afford it. I'm only on a paltry lecturer's salary, you know." Right across campus, I found the same philosophy: academics still in their old mindset of poverty-stricken student. Faded, holed denims and second-hand rusty vehicles abounded everywhere. Conversely, the students looked quite respectable, I thought, if a little "OK yah" in their newly straitened lifestyles.

Of course, that evening when I recounted what the academics had said to me about their so-called paltry lecturers' salaries, the response came quick as a flash: "Yes we know they're all paltry lecturers." Fits of laughter all around.

Back at work, I smiled secretly to myself. The fools! Why was it only I who seemed to have grasped that essential tenet of life? There's no point working to live, spending ever-increasing salaries on ever-increasing mortgages, expense accounts, high society manoeuvring, etc. There are far more satisfying ways to enjoy your life before it's too late and before you don't have any more life to live.

What I could never understand was why on this planet the houses in the most-desirable areas of the world — that is, where it's pleasantly warm, the air is clean, and there are lots of cheap land and houses all around — tend to be cheaper than on tiny, crowded, cold islands like this one. Well, I wasn't going to delve too deeply into the economics of that one; better to grasp the facts as they were, however illogical, and benefit as best I could.

What I can't help but notice, back in this northern clime is the standard attitude of the local urban people, particularly the elderly. Whereas in France, it was always '*bonjour, ça va,*' here it's grumbles all around. I remember the oh-so-familiar attitudes of customers at our now defunct shop: 'I don't suppose you've got one of these?' holding up some tiny, obscure item. It was as if they were so sure you wouldn't have such a thing, they had almost not bothered to ask. Such a contrast to the Americans with their 'shop 'til you drop' philosophy, and their highly definitive all-demanding requirements, so requisite in a totally customer-oriented society. I suppose it's the half-full/half-empty glass philosophy, or even the light at the end of the tunnel/lights of the approaching train mentality.

Still, this was England. We had yet to fully explore the mentality of the French. Let's hope they're prepared for the imminent advent of two Victor Meldrews.

All would soon be revealed.

Last day at work

March came in windy and cold, the sky grey and permanently overcast. Now that I had effectively banished my fear of late arrival at work, I had now taken to walking to work with a set of earphones over my frozen ears, the whole ensemble covered by my warm black Russian Cossack hat. I certainly looked the part, I thought to myself, as I trudged through the frozen wastes to that waste of time that was work at the moment. But at least I could brighten the day by listening to my favourite Radio 4, even if I was forever shouting down that John Humphrys as he continued to harangue the politicians of the day. Certainly there were quite a few passers-by who shook their heads at this crazy English woman tramping the cold pavements at that time of day.

Once at work, I dismantled myself from all those wires and hung my outer gear on the hook that passed as a coat rack in our office. With a sigh I settled into my daily routine, waiting for the usual introductory programmes to become established on my work PC before becoming embroiled in the hundreds of daily emails received from wannabee students from all over the world. As with all PhD hopefuls, they all had the qualifications but were desperately seeking funding. It was the overseas students I felt the most sorry for. The fees were horrendous, on top of which they had to find living costs and travel expenses. Every time I started to read: 'Respectful Madame....', my heart sank. Here was yet another highly qualified overseas student with little hope of achieving all the exorbitant fees needed. As a department we offered one highly prized scholarship fund for such students, but it was so competitive that to fill the six vacancies a year, we received over a thousand applications. But soon, after all these years, I wouldn't need to worry about this any longer. I was more than happy to hand over the reins to my colleagues.

I saw no reason to delay any longer, so handed my notice in at work without so much as a second thought. Never would I have believed that such a momentous event, something I wouldn't have dreamt of doing in my introverted, insecure early years at work, could be accomplished without so much as a backward glance.

The last two months sped by in a dream. For the first time in my working life I didn't have to worry about what time I arrived, what I did or said, for what could they do: sack me? I was leaving anyway!

Ah, what joy. The only thing left to resolve was my farewell speech. Would I throw all those proverbial custard pies? Time would tell. Certainly, there were managers in the past who should be quaking in their boots at all that they had thrown at me over the years. Such temerity I had shown in wanting to improve my station in life! Such a cheek in wanting to rise above the traditional, now obsolete, shorthand-typist level to one of the higher echelons of administratorship. I could hear them all now with malignant schadenfreude. Why can't girls recognise their true level and stay there? I could still hear their disdain when I was studying for an OU degree. I was not even given the time off to take my final exams, even though the venue was our very own university's Great Hall just across the campus from my office, and had to use my precious holiday time. Well, if I was foolish enough to study above my given level…..

Hah!

My final day at work for all time arrived. After much soul-searching and much editing I had prepared my leaving speech, which was to be delivered in the grassy quadrangle situated in the central courtyard of the departmental building. What finally decided me was remembering the wisdom of some past eminent professors, who had said to me: "Don't leave on a sour note. Let people remember you with warmth, not hostility."

I had delivered a few speeches in my life as chairman of a local friendship lodge, so I knew what I wanted to do: speak without notes in a manner that would come over well. And I believe it did. I had started on a light note to put people at their ease: "Looking around at you all, I never realised that it would take so many of you to finally escort me off the premises….," pausing for laughter. On a more serious note I was glad I had remembered phrases from the heart, like: "It's not where people come from, or what they look like that matters in life, just what's in their heart……." It wasn't until I had finished that I noticed my manager had decided to remain absent on my final day of glory — or was it out of feelings of guilt or even fear of what I might say?

Anyway, the applause that echoed and reverberated around the departmental courtyard at the end will remain with me for the rest of my life.

8
In transit: England to France

It's apple-blossom time. White blossoms are exhibiting their finery like ballet-dancers at a ball, twirling their delicate skirts with every sudden gust of wind.

I'll be with you in apple-blossom time
I'll be with you to change your name to mine
One day in May, I'll come and say
Happy's the bride that the sun shines on today...

Well, we're not exactly getting married again, but we're certainly on the brink of a brand new life together. We may be getting on a bit, but we're not too old to feel that first quiver of excitement at the challenges that lie ahead.

It is now a *fait accompli*. We're both officially out of work for the first time in the last forty odd years and we don't care one jot.

I've arranged for the removals firm to collect our furniture out of Alcatraz and I've given them our new address in south-west France. It seems that it is no longer necessary to obtain customs clearance when shipping household effects within the EU. Of course, to do it right we should have employed a company that's a member of the International Federation of Furniture Removers (FIDI). With these sort of companies, you get a guarantee that if a member company fails to fulfil its commitments, the removal is completed at the agreed cost by another company within the federation or your money is refunded. However, H says that their acronym should read International Firm which Rakes in Reams of our Cash, so we've as usual gone for a cheaper option. We nearly went for Grotley's Rubbish, but in the end plumped for O'Flaherty's Travel. After all, as H says, how could he resist their slogan of 'O'Flaherty will get you nowhere!' We have opted for their special cheap offer (oh no) of a part load, where the cost is shared with other deliveries to the same area, but it may mean a longer wait at the other end for the van's arrival *chez-nous*. It may also mean that that precious vase from Aunt Maud that she gave us for our wedding forty years ago could be delivered somewhere else. "Hurrah!" says H. All companies ask that customers make a list of everything to be moved and to give a copy to the removal company. Apparently we should avoid such items as guns, bombs, drugs and pornographic videos…….so that's half our load reduced already.

I've given O'Flaherty detailed instructions of our new address as I know how difficult it is to find once you're surrounded by miles and miles of French fields. So, all that remains is to do a frantic final clean of the flat, cram our few personal belongings from the flat into the back of the car, and return the key to the rental agency. I was determined to clean up well, as I knew that in lettings agents training manuals, the cost of sending in a cleaner for the next tenant was always expected to be deducted from the previous tenant's holding deposit! All would be revealed.

Did I say 'few personal belongings'? For the last hour we've been pushing, shoving, cramming and squeezing, but it's no good. Whichever way we try, there just isn't enough room. Either I go without him indoors or some of it will have to go.

Up aloft, balancing precariously on a rusting old downpipe, sits a member of the ubiquitous English pigeon-brigade. As he looks down disdainfully at us with his beady eye, he suddenly renews with vigour his awful daily serenade of "oo oo oo". That's all we needed as we continued our impossible task.

It's now five o'clock in the morning. The plan had been to get an early start, ahead of all that dratted rush-hour traffic for the last time. However, there's that dratted pigeon again, it's raining and we're standing on the roadside in front of the apartment block, fuming as we get wetter and wetter. In the end, in a rage of stress and anxiety, an indiscriminate medley of clothes is dragged from the boot and slung pell-mell into the universal waste container hiding in the smelly box at the foot of the stairwell. Tramps will have a field day, but there is nothing we can do. It's either that or delay even longer. I had a sudden feeling that if we didn't go now, we never would.

We're off! The car is so heavily laden that I'm sure the front axle will lift off if we ever get some speed going. It's a good job we're still in familiar territory, as the driver hasn't a hope in hell of seeing anything out of the back window. As we pass all those familiar landmarks on the way, we cheerfully wave goodbye, hopefully for the very last time. Bye-bye university, work and stress (with a personal two-fingers to all those who did their utmost to make my life hell on earth), bye-bye traffic……bye-bye England.

It was nice knowing you, but now la *grande aventure* can commence.

As we drive onto the now-familiar Eurotunnel train at Folkestone, we call out to a bemused-looking farmer in a distant field:

"Will the last one out switch off the lights."

PART TWO

LA BELLE FRANCE

9
Our new French house

Yet is a path more difficult before me, and I fear
That in its broken windings we shall need
The chamois' sinews and the eagle's wing
William Wordsworth

Buying a house in France is not a commonplace activity. The French rarely move house, it seems. On the occasions they do, the notaire is there in order to assist both parties in taking the necessary precautions to avoid common and costly errors. For the buyer the notaire's duty is to ensure that you perform the purchase without risk.

So we were informed.

As our appointment was not until the following day, we had time to look around our new village. I desperately needed to take another look to convince myself we were doing the right thing. I knew I wanted the house, but hadn't really explored the surrounding village. Now was the time before we finally sealed the bargain.

So, after breakfast we found ourselves standing in the village square. The morning haze hung like gauze over distant green fields and long-limbed trees stood motionless, their new spring leaves unstirred by even the faintest breeze. But, as our landlady had prophesied, this mist that often shrouds the area at early morn was already beginning to clear slowly from the ground upwards. Paradis de Quercy, to give it its full name, was soon bathed in a warm glow, shafts of translucent sunlight from the clear Spring sky picking out the cream and honey walls of its mediaeval castle and church ramparts. We looked up and shaded our eyes from the suddenly bright light. Perched on the high crenulations was a buzzard. His cold beady eye reminded me of Général de Gaulle. He was looking down on us from his lofty superior position, as if to cast some kind of gallic heavenly judgement on our worthiness, before soaring up to the heavens again in his quest for more succulent prey. Soon, no doubt, after basking in the relative warmth of Paradis de Quercy in the winter, he would be winging north to his favoured cooler summer haunts of Norway and Lithuania.

We walked on. Behind the ancient sandstone castle lay the ever-present Aveyron river, snaking its way through lush green valleys, before falling down sheer rocks into the lower levels beneath. On its Paradis de Quercy stretch, its waters were now cascading rapidly down the weir, churning the wheel of the old watermill underneath the Auberge restaurant, pride of the village.

Later, to cries of '*bon appetit'*, we found ourselves smiling at our fellow diners as we enjoyed a meal whilst sat at fretworked tables dotted underneath a white awning. The menu was simply superb, but after some deliberation we each plumped for the following simple fish meal:

Soupe à l'oignon gratinée
Mousse de Saumon et Câpres
Gratin dauphinois
Plateau de fromages et salade verte
Poires Belle Hélène

Between courses we stared at the plaque on the heavy crépi walls of the restaurant, as if needing further reassurance that this wasn't all a dream:

Restaurant
Cuisine Traditionnelle et inventive
*Terrasse d'*été ombragée
Sur les berges de l'Aveyron
À Paradis de Quercy

The glittering ripples of the waters alongside served to whet our appetites for some local Gaillac wine, as we surveyed the glorious riverside scene. Eventually we plumped for the Renaissance Gaillac label, une appellation contrôl*ée,* a dry white wine of considerable flavour. We felt like a million dollars as we leaned back in our rustic seats and looked out over the river. The cry of a chaffinch alerted us to a distant russet branch as it shook its melange of colourful tail feathers and dipped its pale beak into the cool waters.

Yes, we were doing the right thing. What more could we want?

The following day dawned, bright and crisp. White snowy clouds were drifting across a lazy sky, here and there interspersed by streaks of white misty trails, past reminders of travellers foolish enough to want to go elsewhere.

We made our way over to the notaire's office, picking our way through the many delightful cobbled alleyways. It wasn't far from the B & B, so we didn't need the car. We walked over to the wooden desk and rang the bell. From somewhere deep within the dark interior appeared an elderly lady.

"Oui?"

"Uh, nous sommes venus pour acheter une maison."

"Nom?"

"Green……" I needed to spell it out in French. I frantically tried to remember the correct pronunciation for each letter of our name (somewhat confusedly remembering the German pronunciations I learned at school). But at least our name wasn't Rumpelstiltskin…… A strangled "*Jay, Aire, uh, uh, en"* emerged, hopefully.

"Non. Vous n'avez pas fait un rendez-vous avec le notaire."

This was unbelievable. We had come all this way, removing all traces of our past existence in England, with not a home to our name, and this woman has the temerity to suggest we haven't made an appointment! I could feel my blood pressure rising. Just then, who should enter into the saintly portals but our vendor and his wife. So, we hadn't made a mistake. Their thankful presence showed that we were right.

H whispered to me: "Ask the assistant to ring the agent."

I did so, and she finally agreed, babbling into the phone at a rate of knots. We walked over to the chairs alongside the wall and, along with our vendors, prepared for a long wait. We were going nowhere. Let's face it; we had nowhere to go.

The clock, positioned high up on the wall, ticked on relentlessly, every so often making a singsong chime as it reached each quarter point on the dial. In frustration my eyes wandered around the room, noting the plethora of dusty reference books on a multitude of shelves positioned high up, as if wanting to preclude any potential purchaser from wanting to read them. From this distance, and with my eyesight, I felt that the old and torn leather spines combined with the blurred tooling of the text lettering would hardly attract anyone let alone nervous anxious waiting customers.

It must have been about thirty minutes, but it seemed more like a hundred, when a harried June from the first agency arrived, along with the Dutch agent and his wife, all breathless from their haste.

We shook hands all around whilst the Dutchman apologised for the inconvenience. They didn't know what had happened but had arranged with the notaire's assistant for him to see us after his present appointment. At least that was something. We were all here for the same purpose. Eventually we were all ushered into the saintly presence and negotiations began.

I began to relax a little, realising that this was nothing unusual. *C'est la France*. Bureaucracy at its finest!

As we were buying our new home in joint names, I was surprised that all the final documentation included my maiden name. This seems to be common in France, but it came as quite a shock to see the name I hadn't seen for nearly forty years — in fact, now I come to think of it, the last time was when I signed the marriage register back in 1967.

The procedure in the notaire's office became even more bizarre. Apparently you even have to determine your last will and testament.

"I was rather hoping to live to see the house first…"

"Yes. Me too."

"No, no, no," said both our agents, who were all required to attend the final signing. "The reason is because, unlike in England, on the death of one of the married couple, the estate (including the house) is shared equally between the children of the couple."

"You mean, if she goes first…" he pointed to me, "I don't get the house?" I could see him reflecting on this sudden revelation. "What happens if I don't get on well with our adult children…..?"

I, of course, was also in the same position.

"Yes, indeed," replied our charming Dutchman. "That is why we advise you to add either a *clause tontine* or something similar to the house purchase agreement to ensure that, in such circumstances, the remaining partner inherits the house."

Quite.

My thoughts turned to old American films where an ageing rich lothario, before it's too late, decides to fulfil his lifetime's dream and marry a young, beautiful nubile girl against his family's wishes. I could just picture the scenario whereby all the upwardly-mobile children, long cherishing the dream of inheriting all their father's wealth, suddenly find themselves apparently disinherited by a young blonde bimbo!

It seemed that the French, in their wisdom, put their faith solely in the true bloodline (i.e., the children), rather than the vagaries of a totally unsuitable person you may decide to marry in your dotage.

I wondered aloud what happened to purchasers in France who are not actually married.

"In these cases, there are many difficulties," replied the Dutchman. "Most unmarried couples wish to protect the surviving individual, but they are treated by the taxman like persons who don't have children; in other words, testamentary gifts are subject to as much as sixty per cent tax."

"Just as well we went through with the marriage, then," from him indoors.

"Seemed like a good idea at the time…..," I responded in

similar mode. "Seriously though," I whispered, "I'm glad the house has no more than half an acre. I mean, although it was tempting to buy lots and lots of land, in practice, even if we'd wanted to instal a pool, tennis court or even croquet lawn……(yes, I know)….., you know what you think of gardening back in England, so how would you have maintained it? Or could we cope with living in a jungle?"

"But," he whispered back, "it would have been nice to have more land. Just think of the investment potential."

The other agent, sitting next to me, must have overheard what we were saying as he joined in: "Ah, but you should bear in mind that, should you ever wish to sell, buyers can sometimes be difficult to find, particularly if the asking price by then has trebled with the cost of renovation. Don't forget that although there are plenty of buyers in the below one hundred thousand mark, once you get above two hundred thousand, they become much thinner on the ground. We've just sold a particularly attractive property at that price level, but it took two years to sell."

We were interrupted from this lull in the proceedings by the notaire who coughed and banged his gavel. I felt I was back in front of the hanging judge again.

"Are all parties happy for matters to proceed?"

Nods all round.

The final agreement was then passed to us for each of us to sign every single page, followed by each of the joint vendors. By the time we had each also written the following declaration, our fingers were stiff:

"Je soussigne……….reçonnais avoir été informé que si, contrairement à mes declarations faites dans l'acte, je recours à un prêt, je ne pourrai pas me prévaloir des articles L.312-1 et suivants du code de la consummation."

"What's a *prêt*?" H whispered to me. "I think it's a loan," I whispered back. "It's some sort of declaration that covers them should our promise that we weren't buying the house with loans of any sort prove to be false, leaving them with purchasers who may not be able to complete the deal."

"That's all right, then," he said, remembering our vow that

never again would we be hostages to fortune by loan-sharks masquerading as bank managers.

Thirty minutes later, fingers still stiff from signing, we shook hands with all parties in the room, the vendors slid those all-important keys across the baize table to us, and kisses all round.

Voilà!

What did surprise us was the fact that the vendors followed us to our new house and waited to see if we were satisfied. This would never have happened in England. I could just picture the scene: purchaser, on walking through the door, complaining about the state of the place, the fact the floors hadn't been vacuumed etc. etc. But in our case the house had been left in immaculate condition, empty and ready for our furniture.

The gentlemen kissed the ladies on each cheek three times — the custom in this part of France – and we were suddenly alone. We walked out to the enormous front lawn and looked up at our new home. Fragrant vermillion roses were blooming and entwining lazily around the front *terrasse*, golden yellow roses were spreading their beautiful fragrance up through the open bedroom window and the heady perfume of lavender was everywhere. We stood quietly listening for a moment.

"Can you hear that?" he asked.

"What? I can't hear a thing."

"Exactly! Merveilleuse."

All we needed now was to wait for O'Flaherty's, otherwise we'd be sleeping on the floor that night. Surprisingly, the van arrived within an hour of our obtaining the keys to our new front door. I don't believe it. I expected to have to wait hours. However, all did not run smoothly. Although the enormous van managed to manoeuvre itself down our narrow lane, despite several attempts it did not manage the sharp turn to get through the gate and up our long drive. It was therefore necessary for the two English drivers to *schlep* (hump) each item of our furniture from the van and up the drive. They were not pleased. Neither was I. I hate all our *tzeritzene hosen* (embarrassing personal items) to be exposed for all our neighbours to see. Perhaps I'm being just too anxious. Eventually, all our goods seemed to be delivered satisfactorily and the drivers were waiting around for their tip. This we understood.

We walked down the drive and checked our new postbox for mail. One envelope sat inside, somewhat flyblown from the tiny ants nestling within. I blew them clear of the envelope and slit it open with my thumb. It was from those English agents who rented the flat to us for six months just before we left the country. With a sigh, I resigned myself to the inevitable. Yes: they had deducted money from our holding deposit to cover them for necessary cleaning before letting to another tenant. What did I tell you? It doesn't matter how clean and tidy you leave a place, you *always but always* have to pay for a cleaner to come and re-arrange things and tidy-up. And what a coup for them, knowing that we were hardly likely to rush back home to argue the point with them.

Goodbye England.

We waved the van away up the lane, then arm in arm we wandered in through the mediterranean-blue front door, which matched the array of blue *volets* all around the property. We were now ready to start our new life in earnest.

"No, not in Ernest, in Paradis…."

Some things never change.

10
We need a French bank account

It's now June and I'm starting to panic again, but we have met some English people here who have told us not to worry and that we're not alone. It is pretty common to feel overwhelmed when you have recently moved to a new country, they tell me, especially if you don't speak the language fluently and have lost the regular support structure of family and friends. Of course relatives back home might still be on the end of the phone or email, but when they are not going through the same experiences as you it can be hard for them to understand and offer practical support.

You can say that again.

The first thing we needed to do was open a French bank account. Everything you do here seems to rely on that all-important Euro cheque-book, so we pushed this job to the top of our agenda. I read that you can open a bank account in France whether you're a resident or a non-resident, but it's best to do this in person.

There is a *Crédit Agricole* branch fifteen kilometres away which our new friends recommended. It is a well-known bank and generally respected, so we motored over there. We had been warned that we needed lots of identification and paperwork from our English bank, so we took everything we could think of, other than the kitchen sink.

We learned that the normal account for day-to-day transactions in France is a current or cheque account (*compte courant* or *compte de cheques*), as in the UK. However, it's illegal in France for banks to pay interest on current accounts, which was a blow as we had been used to this bonus from our English building society. Two hours later we had transferred money from our English building society, set up a current account and a guarantee that we would receive our new Euro cheque book and debit card within the next two weeks, so we were on our way. However, we noted that our bank card wasn't a cheque guarantee card, as these don't exist in France. The bank manager showed us a sample cheque book and pointed out the numerous printed slips stapled inside. These are called *relevé d'identité bancaire* or *RIB*, pronounced 'reeb.' Each slip contains details of name, personal account and bank codes, and it is common practice to send these slips to anyone who requires them, for example when setting up utility services at home. This seemed strange to us, and our first response was that we were used to keeping such details private. But when in Rome....

As we walked back out into the fresh air again, we glanced at the *distributeur* on the wall outside the bank, as we knew we would be making much use of that for weekly cash withdrawals.

When the time came to write our first cheque, it still needed a lot of concentration. Things were no longer as easy as in the UK. French cheques require brainpower over several stages. First you need to correctly translate into French the amount to pay, then remember what to write in each blank space on the cheque, then work out how to spell the amount, whilst all the time maintaining some semblance of a relationship with the other person and a sense of self as a capable adult! In other words, don't descend into a gibbering wreck at the very first stage.

The main difference we found with French cheques is that the first line is for writing in words the amount you are spending, rather than the shop to whom you are paying it. When writing the figures in the box on the right, the number seven is crossed to avoid confusion with the number one, written with a tail and looking like an uncrossed seven to many foreigners. Beware also of French fours, as they can look like nines (which are written with a curly tail) or twos. The other difference is people use a comma to separate whole numbers and decimals (e.g. 789 euros and 12 cents is written

789,12), whereas a full-stop or a space is used to separate millions and thousands (e.g. 1.234.567,89 is 1 million, 234 thousand, 567 euros and 89 cents). Wishful thinking!

I also noticed that each cheque has our home address written at the base, so there's no running away. Also, the bank left me in no doubt that to overdraw our current account, even unintentionally, was illegal and liable to a hefty fine or even jail. We had been warned! What I couldn't understand when shopping at the local supermarket was why so many locals paid by cheque and not by debit card. Our first bank statement gave us the reason why. Debit cards or *cartes bleues* entail a monthly charge of around four euros! This seemed hefty to us, but I still didn't want to be without it so resolved to carry on as we were for the time being.

I was coming to the slow realisation that when everything is new and you are on a steep learning curve, it can often feel as if you are getting nowhere. What began as a great adventure starts to become hard work.

Everyone tells me that I must stop generalising over everything and think of the positive things that we want in our new life. What was it we really wanted? We already realised that even simple things were likely to take us a lot longer in France than they did in the UK, but the important thing was that we should be aware of what we had already achieved.

One of our new English friends asked whether we had a joint bank account and whether she could see our cheque book. We were puzzled but had nothing to hide so showed her.

"Ah, that's good," she said, "you are listed as M. *ou* Mme. You probably didn't realise, but there is a big difference between how they have printed your name on each cheque." Apparently if our cheque book had said 'M. *et* Mme' then on the ultimate death of one of us, the remaining account holder would be unable to validate the transaction by signing, meaning the account would be frozen until further notice. In that event, the surviving person would then have to wait for the inheritance to be ruled on in order to benefit from their share. Thank goodness, then, that we were listed as 'M. ou Mme', so that each transaction can be requested by either of us, whatever the situation in the future.

There were so many pitfalls to this living in a foreign country!

Would we survive it all?

H turned to me and said: "I know why we took out a joint account….it's because of my sprained wrist!"

"Oh God."

11
Apéritifs

Spring time in the French countryside. The view from the window of our salon is simply glorious. Long fronds of golden mimosa waft their heady perfume in through the open French doors, whilst our new cottage garden replete with masses of crimson fuchsia and fragrant lavender invites myriads of exotic butterfly and insect.

During those long cold winter days last year in England, I had long dreamed of what I would like to do on arrival in our new village. It was very important to me to try to integrate into French life. I hated the idea of being part of some expat English clique, so wanted to do all I could to change that image of the Englishman or woman abroad.

So what better way than to invite our new neighbours onto the patio for an apéritif? There were just four other houses in our lane, so the plan was that I would walk to each one, introduce myself and invite them for, say, next Tuesday morning.

We looked at each other. "You'd better do it," said he. "I wouldn't know what to say….and even if I worked it out in the dictionary, I probably wouldn't understand the answer. No, dear, it's better if you do it."

"Yes, right," I replied, suddenly nervous at the prospect. What would I say? With paper and pencil at the ready, I worked out a few possibilities. I soon realised that it's no good trying to translate directly from our English phrases. Far better to say something simple, something that would be readily understandable and easy to pronounce.

With mounting trepidation, I walked to our nearest neighbour and banged on the door. No response, but I could hear a lawnmower in the back. Plucking up courage I walked around the side of the bungalow and approached an elderly man sitting on one of those ride-on mowers. He was wearing one of those Bill and Ben sun hats, but with rather elegant matching long shorts and shirt. I suddenly thought *I do hope he isn't the gardener*, but he seemed rather too old to still be in employment and certainly too well-dressed, so hoped for the best.

"Excusez-moi, monsieur...."

He turned off the ignition and jumped down onto the springy grass.

"Oui?" puzzled.

"Um. Nous venons déménager – c'est la maison avec le portail bleue là-bas," hoping that he understood my accent and that we were the new people in the blue house over the road. Slightly more confident, I continued: "Nous voudrions vous inviter et votre femme pour un apéritif chez-nous mardi prochaine à onze heurs."

He thought for a moment, weighing up our invitation for next Tuesday and said: "Ah, malheureusement je pense que ce n'est pas possible mardi. Il faut aller à Montauban mardi. Mercredi est d'accord."

Foolishly I hadn't thought that the day might be inconvenient. I had struggled so hard with the French that it hadn't occurred to me there might be problems. But at least he was the first neighbour I had approached, so it wasn't too late to change our plans.

"D'accord. À mercredi à onze heurs. À bientôt."

This done, I walked smartly out of his drive and turned my face towards the next challenge, the farmer further up the lane. A harassed-looking woman of about forty-five was watering vegetables in her front garden plot. She was wearing one of those ubiquitous black and white spotted aprons that are common in this part of the world, the whole ensemble tied several times around her waist. At my approach she looked up suddenly and winced as an apparent sudden attack of sciatica made her hand fly to the small of her back in sympathy. I coughed and introduced myself, like before, frantically trying to remember my French invitation speech. Just in time I remembered to substitute 'mercredi' instead of Tuesday. She looked puzzled for a moment, then suddenly recognising my no-doubt heavily-accented words, understanding shone forth. She called to the barn at the back, and a man evidently her husband emerged. We shook hands and I learned that she was called Josephine and her husband was Jean-Paul. All men around these parts seemed to be called Jean something or other it seemed. From their smiles I gathered that they would be pleased to come round next Wednesday.

Bon.

Now for the last two neighbours.

These visits went quite well, my mind struggling to remember everyone's names and which names lived in which house.

Thankfully I returned home, pleased that all the invitations had now been issued. I told the story to him indoors.

"Did you shake hands?"

"Yes," puzzled.

"Ah. That means that they are still treating you as a stranger. You'll know when they've accepted you — you'll get three kisses from each of them, especially the men."

I gathered that he himself was looking forward to the time when he would be giving three kisses to all the women. I don't think his invitation would be extended to the men somehow.

Over the following few days I started to panic over what we could offer our guests. It was difficult enough back in England, but here? What did the French normally do on such occasions? Finally I resolved to keep it simple. I had seen in the supermarché some tiny pieces of toast advertised as suitable for canapés. All I would need to do would be to spread alternate slices with cream cheese and cucumber, and smoked salmon.

"What we having to drink?" said our resident alcoholic.

"What do you suggest? You're the expert."

"Well, the French always seem to like Pastis, and I've still got that bottle of Scotch we brought with us." He looked slightly discomforted at the thought of giving away his prized whisky, but needs must.

At the thought of canapés, I well remember when I had sent him indoors round to the corner shop for such an item, only to see him return with a can of peas!!

Ever the comedian.

Wednesday dawned cloudy with a few spots of rain. *Oh no!* We'll have to have the party indoors. I looked around. It should be O.K. Last week had seen the arrival of one of our special purchases: a heavy solid real-oak table with eight matching chairs which we'd bought from a friendly store in Montauban called *Monsieur Meuble*. The shop name doesn't translate well in English. I mean, I'm sure we wouldn't call a shop 'Mr. Furniture.' But, looking now at our new table and chairs, we felt really at home. No French home worth its salt is without a large wooden table as the centrepiece of the salon for that all-important *bien manger*, so now we were all set, as the Americans say.

I spent the morning shouting at him indoors, who eventually retreated out of the way to the barn (his very own potting-shed) whilst I prepared the canapés. I arranged everything around our new table and put the bottles of drink and glasses in the centre. I had decided against wine, because I felt it would be like offering coals to Newcastle. Was that the phrase? Anyway, whichever wine I bought might not meet the locals' standards, so I decided in the end to offer them our Scotch as the pièce de la résistance, with the Pastis of course, some fruit juice and a jug of water.

As the clock ticked towards eleven, the heavens opened. Typical! Still, we should be O.K. inside, once our guests had negotiated their way up our long shingle and gravel drive. But, what on earth was I going to say? Would I have enough French to keep the conversation going? I had gathered from first meeting them that not one of them spoke any English at all. Well, that would concentrate the mind as we searched for the right words to say.

I looked again around the salon. I know. I would ask their opinion on our plans for renovating the kitchen. My experience of life had taught me that people always like to be asked their opinion on things. It makes them feel important and puffs up their confidence no end. Yes, that's what I would do. Our kitchen was the worst room in the house at the moment, without a doubt. It was a tiny room, which led off the main salon. All it contained in essence was an old white sink and a gas stove. That was it. No worktops, no room for a table, nothing.

Being typically English and having watched all those renovation programmes on TV, what we planned to do was comprehensive and grand. We would knock down the two walls which fronted onto the salon, opening up the space so that we could instal what they call here '*une cuisine américaine.*' The new units would run right the way across the new back wall as part of our bigger, lighter salon.

A timid tapping on our front door woke me out of my reverie. Our first guests had arrived. Help! I asked him indoors: "Do I look all right?"

"Yeah, great."

With considerable relief I countered "It's wonderful what make-up can do."

To which the instant reply "Well, why don't you wear any then?"

Nothing much changes. I wiped my sweating hands on the back of my summer dress and rushed to open the door. It was Franck and Marie-Therese from over the road.

"Bonjour, Franck. Bonjour Marie-Therese," I said smiling, ushering them inside out of the rain. "Entrez, entrez." They entered hesitantly, looking around, nervous at being the first to arrive.

The resident alcoholic stepped forward.

"Voulez-vous un Pastis?" hopefully.

Franck looked solemnly at the drink on the table. Suddenly his eyes sparkled at sight of the whisky.

"Ah, Johnny Walker!" smacking his lips in appreciation.

"No, that's not my name…"

Surprisingly, in heavy English accent: "I like whisky, if you please," holding out his glass in anticipation. So he did speak some English, after all – when the temptation was great enough.

By now the other neighbours had started to trickle in, literally, wiping their feet free of the mud trails as they went. It appeared that all the other men were called Jean something. There was Jean-Paul, the farmer, Jean-Phillipe and Jean-Marc. And much to our resident alcoholic's disgust, they all wanted whisky. As the party wore on, I could see him eyeing the shrinking whisky levels with much despondency.

All this time I was doing my best to act the smiling, confident hostess with the mostest. I took the canapés round from person to person, as everyone stood in groups round the table. When the food and drink seemed to have diminished somewhat, I waved airily at our current shambles of a kitchen and asked a few of the Jeans what they thought of our renovation plans. This tested my French to the limit. But they seemed to understand. They stood, stroking their chins pensively, whilst they looked first at one wall, then the other.

Franck asked in his little bit of English: "What is it you do here?"

"Well," I replied, struggling with the technical French, "we plan to knock down these two walls, and I understand it will be necessary to put in an RSJ...." Unfortunately there didn't seem to be an equivalent word for RSJ in French, well certainly not one that our dictionary could possibly include, but I think he understood anyway. He confided to H that he would bring over a current catalogue from *Brico Depot*, the big DIY store in Montauban. It would prove a treasure-trove – not just for the items it advertised but as a technical French dictionary for all those DIY items we needed that weren't in the standard English:French books issued by booksellers. On every page there was a picture above the item, with the relevant French term beneath. Perfect, and free too! H flipped through it. "Ah, un tournevis," he said, pointing to the screwdrivers. Clearly there would be no problem with his French when he wanted to buy DIY items, but if I sent him out to buy eggs……..

The women wandered over.

"Ah, une cuisine américaine!" they exclaimed. "Ce sera superbe."

Success at last! I was certain that the reason so many dilapidated properties remained unsold in France was that the French themselves preferred modern building methods and modern plumbing. They didn't seem to have the heart to undertake all the renovation that would be required. Give them the choice between an old run-down *maison de maître* and a newly-built detached house, they would plump for the latter every time. But the English? No. Maybe it's because we have been starved of our historical heritage by the wholesale demolition that continues in every town and village throughout the UK. Shame really. Historians have always said that to know ourselves, we need to know our past. But how can we, when our buildings are continually pulled down?

After our guests had finished their ponderings over our kitchen plans, I showed the women round the rest of the house. I don't know why, but it is always the women who like to look at things like that. I tried to explain about what we hoped to do to the old bathroom. There was an unfortunate 70's sunken bath, which we didn't like. At first sight him indoors had laconically observed: "It's a hole waiting to fall into." And I had to agree, thinking of our needs in the decades to come.

Our lady guests all agreed with our plans to build a walk-in shower, complete with six therapeutic massage jets or *buses* — great for the lower back. Our plans called for us to build a new tiled brick wall to one side. Although this would be a messy job, we preferred this to installing one of those wobbly plastic shower cubicles. It should be easier to keep clean — none of that messy black mould building up - and would make use of the excellent water pressure round here. I don't know why in this day and age you can't get sufficient water pressure in England.

Soon it was time for the party to come to a close. Our

guests had by now become much more relaxed if the laughter and jokes were anything to go by. Or was it the whisky talking?

Anyway, how do you think we knew the party had been a success? Yes, you're right. Kisses on both cheeks three times.

Voilà!

12
Communication and Panic

Spring is a wonderful season. The birds are singing, the trees have changed from their winter dull brown to shiny new greenery and everywhere is still and expectant, awaiting what summer will bring.

But it was so quiet. We felt eager for news, anything to fill this unaccustomed void in our daily lives. There's nothing like moving house, home and country to make you realise that you are suddenly out of touch from everyone. We needed a phone and fast. But how to get one if we can't call the telephone company? There was absolutely no point in my reading that France has the third largest telephone network in the world and that over ninety percent of French households have a telephone if I couldn't obtain one myself. I started to panic. What if we needed to call a doctor, ambulance, fire brigade....my subliminal neuroses were on high alert.

What to do?

I wandered around to our local friendly pharmacist and asked his advice. Fortunately, most pharmacists in France are highly educated and this one spoke English well. He kindly agreed to phone France Télécom for us and explained the problem, holding the phone to his ear whilst he sorted through a pile of dog-eared prescriptions on his desk. Clearly he was highly skilled at multi-tasking. *Should have been a woman*, I thought. Every so often he would pause from his unintelligible gabble to take his phone from his ear and ask me various questions. Did our house have a telephone socket? What were the details of the vendors, etc.

With a hearty voilà, he crashed the phone down and turned back to me.

"You must go to the office of France Télécom and take with you documents to prove you are the owner of the property."

"What sort of documents?"

"An electricity bill?"

"No. We haven't been here long enough yet."

"Oh, O.K., then you should take your confirmation of purchase or *attestation d'acquisition* that you should have received from the Notaire, together with your passport. It's good that your house already has a telephone line, because if it hadn't...*mon Dieu*...it would have cost you a lot of money to get a new line installed, trenches dug etc. And you should also take a note of the kind of phone sockets you have in your house."

I thanked the pharmacist and we dashed to the nearest large town to find the phone shop. We knew that we could probably buy a phone handset from LeClerc or several other large hypermarkets, but we concentrated first on getting our new number and line established.

After our usual trauma of asking directions from all-comers, we at last found the shop, and wonder of wonders they weren't about to stop for lunch. But there was a long queue, so we heaved a sigh, picked up what looked like a lottery ticket from the counter and settled down to await our turn. Three hours later, him of limited patience shouted out: "We weren't planning on taking a day's holiday here you know." But no-one understood anyway.

Eventually, before we had lost the will to live, our turn at last came. I told the assistant our difficulties and she told us of the English-language telephone information service.

"But how are we supposed to do this if we haven't actually got a phone?"

She gave a noncommittal shrug. No doubt her thoughts flew to public phone booths but anyone who has ever tried to use one of these in a foreign country would have comments of their own. After we had spoken some more, the assistant tapped some information onto a screen and very soon we were actually given our very own new number. Then the previous occupant's account was transferred to us as from our moving-in date. There are always unscrupulous people who continue to use their old account at your expense. We had been warned. Apparently in France it isn't possible to simply take the number of the previous occupants, so a new number was *de rigeur*.

I then asked about Broadband. Trouble is I've heard that the electricity supply in many rural areas like ours is somewhat temperamental, to say the least. Apparently it is not unusual for the lights to flicker and occasionally go off and come back on again intermittently, i.e. just long enough to crash the computer! I'd read somewhere that un *parafoudre* was *de rigeur*, but didn't know what such a thing was. Yet another thing to ask about then. Because power cuts are fairly frequent in our area, particularly during thunder storms, we determined that we would keep torches, candles and maybe even a gas lamp handy. "Just like in the scouts," said H. "Then all our excitement will be in-tense….."

Whilst we waited for the Télécom girl to finish tapping in all our details, my mind reflected on the other utilities *cheznous*. As far as gas is concerned, our new house unfortunately has one of those *citerne* gas tanks sitting around the back. I say unfortunately because I don't like them. I can't help but think we are sleeping next to a ticking time-bomb every night. But people laugh when I tell them of my fears. They are safer than any other method, I'm told, because there are built-in safety valves. I remain unconvinced, but suppose I'll get used to it. They are common in rural France, where mains gas isn't yet installed. We needed to set up a *prélévement*, direct debit, to pay Total Gaz every month. This includes the rental of the *citerne* plus an estimate of our gas consumption, regularised at the end of each year, as in the UK.

As far as electrical items are concerned, I'd brought over a new PC from England. I had wondered at the time whether it might be better to buy one in France but decided against it. As an old-style touch typist, I needed the familiarity of an English *QWERTY* keyboard to be able to type at anything like my old speeds. I couldn't cope with learning a new set of automatic hand-movements at my age. You can't teach old dogs new tricks.

When the Télécom girl had finished tapping in all our details, I discussed the PC problem with her. In the end we purchased a separate ADSL line from that of the phone so that we could use the computer at the same time as using our new fixed phone line. All that then remained was to buy two new handsets, one for the salon and one for the bedroom and we were all set. We noticed that the standard French phone connector is a large block with a single blade-like plug, so we bought a special double adaptor that would take both the phone and the PC connector.

Once home again, and new handsets plugged in and working, I began on my new set of worries. What to do in an emergency? Franck told me that it's always best to call the Fire number (18) as the *pompiers* handle the widest range of emergency situations, including road accidents and natural disasters, and will notify an ambulance or police if they believe the situation warrants it. As in the UK, all calls to emergency numbers are free from both public and private telephones.

I was intrigued to hear that our local, rural *pompier* station was manned by twenty-four men and women volunteers. It seems that over ninety percent of France's *pompiers* are volunteers because France's paid professions are reserved for the major population centres. In villages like ours it is not uncommon for sons to continue the work of their fathers, whether in the butcher's shop, the farm or in this case, the *pompiers*. It sounded like the apprentice schemes the UK used to run years ago before the practice died out for one reason or another. But here in rural France, every small local private enterprise, whether it be electrician, builder, painter or plumber, sports a van carrying one older man or woman, with a young apprentice paid to learn the hands-on skills of the elder. If only……

Anyway, it seems that anyone aged seventeen to fifty-five can train to be a *pompier*. They have around three hundred hours of training at the start, topping these up with regular refresher and up-to-date courses. Franck told me that our local *pompier* covers nine communes, three in each of the départements adjoining our village, although the over-riding authority is in the home départment.

"But how are they paid?" I had asked Franck.

He replied that major funding is provided from a departmental budget, which whilst never enough, provides for a very well-equipped station, with several specialist vehicles designed to fight fires in buildings or forests, provide water-borne rescue, get cats out of pot holes or hornets out of trees…

No permanent staff is maintained at the station, but an up-to-date radio system enables the watch to be called out at any time. It often happens that customers have to be prepared for their plumber to down tools at a moment's notice — not for a tea break but to answer his *pompier* bleep.

I wondered if the influx of foreign residents like us had made things more difficult as often they have a poor grasp of the language. Franck replied that it can cause problems when an emergency arises and the person is unable to respond clearly to the *pompier's* questions. It was suggested that one of the best ways to overcome this (apart from learning to improve their spoken French of course) would be for some of our younger compatriots to consider actually joining the *pompiers* themselves. That way they would integrate wonderfully into village life and provide a service to all the residents.

I couldn't help but ask Franck why the *pompiers* devote so much time and energy to such a demanding pastime. He explained that it was just a public service to their fellow villagers, and to each of them: "*sauver une vie, c'est genial.*"

To build on all this useful advice, I realised I needed a telephone directory which would give me all the information I needed. I tried telephoning France Télécom again. Eventually, after listening to several minutes of irritating advertising music, and being asked to 'tappez un', I managed to reach a real person.

"Uh. J'ai besoin du directeur," hopefully. I didn't know the

French word for directory.

"Comment?"

I repeated my question.

I couldn't understand the girl's apparent hysteria until later when Franck told me that the French word for telephone directory is *un annuaire*. Completely different word!

I had apparently told the girl that I had need of the Director!

13
I told you I was ill!

For a happy marriage
The husband should be deaf
And the wife blind
Old Occitan proverb

Summer must have finally arrived. Our ancient ventilator fan has been moved into the bedroom, ready and willing to crank into life when perspiration in the middle of the night reaches that point of no return.

He who never went to the doctor back home, when everything was free, has now decided he should get his left leg checked out. It must have been whilst wearing his new French shorts that I bought from the open air *marché* in nearby Caussade that brought him to this momentous decision. He has been limping for more years than I care to remember, resulting in one leg having become wasted and thinner than the other one. There's nothing like exposing all that flesh to reveal life's imperfections. I had a brother who once said that everyone should be like him and not wear glasses, as he didn't want to see everyone's spots and pimples in all their red and gory detail. But there we were. The shorts definitely revealed H's leg problem to one and all, so a solution needed to be found.

When we were originally contemplating moving to France – or rather when I had decided and H had reluctantly agreed – I had managed to persuade the medical people at the Centre for Non-Residents in Newcastle upon Tyne that I should be issued with their E106 form. This was no mean feat, as I was pushed from pillar to post trying to get through to the correct office.

Eventually I managed to persuade them that I had been paying full national insurance contributions for nearly thirty years and surely I was entitled to something? But, of course, because I was yet to reach the magical age when I would qualify for a full pension, all they could promise me was an E106 form.

"But, what am I supposed to do with it?" I asked, expecting a rude reply.

"We will send you two copies of the E106. You need to take both forms to your local sickness insurance office. Do not fill in any part of the form yourself (on pain of death!). The foreign authority will then complete part B of both forms. They will send one copy to us to confirm registration and will keep a copy themselves. Once you have registered with the foreign authority, they will deal with any claim you make for help with medical costs. They can also tell you what you are entitled to."

"But, you told me that my E106 will run out in January 07 – that's eleven months before I reach sixty. What will we do then?"

"When your E106 certificate runs out, you must make enquiries with your local sickness insurance office about the possibility of joining their sickness scheme. Then, when you actually reach sixty, you can apply to us for our form E121."

Another form, aargh!

I put the phone down, my head reeling. So that was all there was to it, then! We didn't even know where our 'local sickness insurance office' was, let alone how to ask about all this in our halting French.

I decided that the most appropriate place to ask was our local friendly pharmacie, where the helpful owner spoke some English. He told us that the office we needed was in Montauban, the capital town of our region. We thanked him and studied the map. As with all the places we needed, it was situated more than fifty miles away. This was proving the case for everything.

Once I received the all-important forms from Newcastle, we filled up the car and prepared for a long haul. As usual on our journeys we took several wrong turns, screeched via hand-brake turns off many a private piece of farmland before we took the inevitable scenic route to Montauban. The traffic in the city reminded us of back home. Narrow roads, parked cars, no time to stop and look before receiving gesticulations and impatient horns. Before coming here I had led a very sheltered life, but have now learned phrases, arm movements and swear words that I would rather not repeat.

By now our watches showed the inevitable: eleven fifty-five. Too late. No wonder French restaurants do such a roaring trade every lunch-time. Everything shuts (except restaurants) for at least two hours every weekday, just when you manage to find the place you're looking for. There was only one thing to do. We walked into a restaurant and ordered lunch.

Later on, the afternoon proved to us what we had always suspected: the French are a nation of form-fillers. Eventually, I was issued with *un attestation* from the *Caisse Primaire d'Assurance Maladie* (CPAM) attesting to the fact that we were both now eligible for French medical benefits. It seemed that in practice, all French citizens pay up front for their medical costs and receive some back. The normal ratio is one hundred percent up front, and five days later, seventy percent of the cost is refunded directly to your French bank account. We still didn't understand when we might receive our carte vitale, that all-important card that would give us credibility in our new country, but in the meantime I suppose the *attestation* will have to do. Mind you my inner neuroses were working non-stop. I could visualise that nightmare scenario of our lying in the road somewhere waiting for the ambulance to arrive, then groggily trying to explain to the trauma team just why we hadn't a carte vitale but that we had got a vital piece of paper that was probably in my handbag somewhere!

Of course, if we hadn't been residents and merely visiting the country, we could have applied for a CEAM card, which gives visitors the benefits of European-wide health insurance. But we had to come to terms with it. We were now *bone-fide* residents and must deal with the issues involved.

On the plus-side, it was clear that the standard of hospital treatment in France is second to none, and we were told there are virtually no waiting lists for operations or hospital beds. Apparently public and private medicine operate alongside one another with no difference in the standard of care between them. Everyone tells us that the quality of health care and facilities in France is among the best in the world, and much private treatment costs considerably less than back home. If ever we develop cataracts, for example, the cost of private treatment would be around nine hundred pounds sterling here, compared with three thousands pounds in the UK. Enough said.

However, our neighbour Franck told us that la France has long been a nation of hypochondriacs, famously satirised by Molière in *Le Malade Imaginaire*. He told us that he reckoned the French visit their doctors more often than most other Europeans and buy large quantities of medicines, health foods and vitamin pills. This must be why, in nearly every run-down dilapidated village we have driven through, the pharmacie looks the most modern, expensive building in the place.

H looked thoughtful. The French must be hypochondriacs; I mean, everywhere I look are adverts for Piles.

"No!" I told him horrified. "Those aren't adverts for haemorrhoids; *piles* is the French word for batteries!" I just knew that this foreign language thing would get us into trouble.

When Franck told us that the incidence of heart disease in France is among the lowest in the world because of the high consumption of red wine, my resident alcoholic's face lit up. Well, it would, wouldn't it?

We both wondered, though, why the NHS couldn't operate in the same manner as the French health service. It seems obvious to everyone except the UK government that the increasing size of the population can no longer sustain a completely free health service. Some sort of charge needs to be levied on all wage-earners. We thought long and hard about the difficulties we had always experienced with English hospitals. The problem seems to lie not in the staff, who always appear surprisingly cheerful in the circumstances, but with the fabric of hospital buildings built in another time with a different set of values. No longer are staff in English hospitals prepared to scrub floors on their hands and knees, preferring modern polishing machines instead. Hospital clinicians seem conditioned to rely on modern antibiotics to kill germs absorbed internally by their patients, rather than the preventative, old-style carbolic administered liberally on floors and walls to disinfect the building rather than the patient. I just don't know why the British put up with such a system. Closing all the old Victorian hospitals and building new, purpose-built buildings capable of maintaining high levels of surgical cleanliness would be a start. The hospitals everyone loves are not the bricks and mortar that hold them together, but the people who actually serve within them. These caring people will still be there in newer, cleaner and more hygienic surroundings. It was the very least staff should expect and what patients deserve, particularly in times of crisis. And if all this requires wage-earners to contribute more, then so be it. It would be worth it.

I shook my head from all this past reverie and put my mind to the job now in hand. We had the French *attestation* so went along to our local doctor in the next village. His office was situated on the *Place de la République*, over the railway line with its frightening red and white barriers permanently at half-mast, over the picturesque bridge shading the river *Seye*, and then left at the little lane by the expensively lit pharmacie.

In the *Salle d'attente* were seated three other people, all elderly. We entered, wishing them all a *bonjour*. We refrained from the usual *ça va*? because clearly if they were all right, they wouldn't have been there. We looked around for a receptionist, but evidently such an officious person, so beloved back home, wasn't required here. We waited. Soon, the doctor breezed in, issued *bonjours* to us all, then welcomed the next in line into his surgery.

I tried to make polite conversation with the lady sitting on my right.

"Monsieur le docteur, il est un bon docteur?"

"Mais oui," shaking her head at such a stupid question.

I shut up and concentrated on translating the several posters pinned to the walls. As I was neither pregnant nor likely to be suffering from Aids, I didn't bother attempting to read further. When the time eventually came for us to go in, I shook hands with the doctor and explained as best I could that I had come as translator for my husband. He nodded and ushered us into his surgery.

"What has brought you to my surgery this morning?" he enquired politely, whilst punching up some details on his PC.

"Our Citroën C4!" said H, quick as a flash.

Nothing wrong with his humour then.

The doctor looked puzzled, as well he might. However, we have hit upon a useful introductory phrase, which always seems to work. "J'ai mal au……," pointing to the offending part of the body. Soon the offending leg was being prodded, pummelled and the knee hit with a hammer. The doctor looked, then gravely pronounced:

"C'est normal pour un homme de votre âge."

"But, my other leg is just the same age, and that one doesn't hurt."

The doctor grunted several times, making copious notes into a file, before telling me that it was best if we sought a second opinion at the local *Hôpital Chartreuse* in yet another town, Villefranche de Rouergue.

"Why do we need a second opinion, when we don't know the first yet?" said he logically.

"Shh," said I resignedly.

The *Hôpital Chartreuse* proved clean, friendly and efficient. I had decided, whilst there, to take up the offer for me to have a mammogram. The French health service, rather like the NHS, invites all ladies over fifty to have a free test and as I had undergone this procedure several times in the UK I didn't think it would be a problem. However, I had forgotten that tiny problem of language.

"Please fill in this form," said the receptionist.

I glanced quickly at it, but was puzzled.

"Why does it ask me for the name of my daughter? How did you know I had a daughter?"

"I don't understand, madame."

"See, here," said I pointing to the first line. "*Nom de jeune fille...*"

"No," she explained resignedly. "We need you to put the name *you* had before you were married."

I felt foolish. And the feeling persisted right into the consulting room. The nurse gabbled something quickly before leaving the room. *Did she say I was supposed to undress? What if she didn't say that and then I am led in my nakedness along a public corridor? Oh God, why ever did we come to a foreign country...*

But once I had at last finished with my radiology, and I was thankfully pronounced fit and well, we proceeded to the Physiology Department, where H's treatment proceeded much better. The Korean doctor we saw there was charm personified. I explained as best I could H's leg problem, furnishing the doctor with the usual difficult to read note from our own doctor. He got straight down to business, asking if the patient could lie down on the narrow, short (!) bed whilst he did several tests on H's nerves and muscles. At some point the doctor unravelled a long cable with a needle on the end. I thought I'd better say something.

"Uh, mon mari n'aime pas les aiguilles." This translates medically as either 'my husband has a low pain threshhold' or more realistically "my husband is a coward." Either way, the doctor seemed to catch on straight away. He told me that as soon as he was about to puncture the patient's foot with the long needle, I should divert his (not the doctor's) attention. I wasn't sure how I was going to do this, but waited for him to nod, before suddenly coughing. My cough was followed instantly by a howl of pain from the unfortunate patient.

Voilà!

The doctor said that in his professional opinion the difficulties with the leg stemmed from problems in the lower back and the fact that H wasn't getting any younger. I translated. To which H replied: "it's not younger I want to get, but older…!"

Anyway, the doctor pronounced that the problem with the leg was nothing too serious that could not be corrected by the purchase of a bicycle.

"See," I told H. "It's what I've always thought . He says you're to get on your bike!"

14
Bruno

Knick-knack-paddy-wack
Give a dog a bone
This old man came rolling home
Old nursery rhyme of unknown origin

Thirty years ago when the children were small, we had a gorgeous pedigree Cavalier spaniel called Brandy. With her enormous soft eyes she was a beautiful creature but, probably because of much in-breeding, was of limited intelligence.
However, in Brandy's latter years I had by then returned to full-time work but always felt guilty at having to leave the dog inside for most of the day. Himself always seemed to hanker after a dog like the one he had as a child; one that had a bit of personality, intelligence and big enough to suit our new wide-open spaces.

So, one sunny day, several months after we had arrived in France, we decided that we would very much like to give a dog a good home with us. After asking our neighbours, we soon discovered that for this area, there was only one place to look: the local SPA (Société Protectrice des Animaux) in Montauban.

Although France is a nation of dog-lovers with around seventeen dogs to every hundred people, many French dogs are kept outdoors and some are almost permanently penned. We had to admit we have never seen anyone in our village actually walk their dogs, and we knew that many people, especially the farmers, kept them merely for practical purposes, to guard their homes or to catch vermin.

But we are English, and you know what that means. The dog will probably be treated by me as a grandchild-substitute and probably hugged to death. Anyway, once the idea took route, I was ready and eager to go and buy one. He wasn't so sure but once I'd got an idea in my head…..

He did the driving, I was chief navigator *comme d'habitude*. This meant that we kept to the right side of the road but that we usually took the scenic route. Today was no exception. Many were the puzzled *fermiers* in the middle of nowhere who were accosted with the question: "Où est le chenil pour chiens?" But eventually, after much reversing and skidding on obscure farm tracks, the dogs literally found us: we heard the barking from afar. As we approached, the sound became louder and louder. God, there must have been hundreds of the poor creatures in there.

We parked outside and clanged open the heavy metal gate. Madame was inside the entrance hut, inputting data onto a screen. Technology seems to have infiltrated just about everywhere and appears in the most unlikely of places, like right here. My first question: 'Parlez-vous anglais?' usually meets with a polite 'Non, d*ésolé*.' This was no exception. But in situations like this, with the two of us as likely paying customers, it's amazing what sign language and combined efforts can do to effect a comprehensive understanding.

"Uh, je cherche un chien."

"Oui. Va devant, je te suis."

"What did she say?"

"Not sure, so let's go ahead and she'll probably follow us."

We followed the noise and soon were faced with the most heartrending sight. Dozens of small cages, each housing about six dogs of single sex, each dog jumping up and wagging frantically as we passed. It felt that each dog was saying to me: "Take me, take me." And I wanted to, desperately. But I knew that the practical side would win in the end. We could probably only cope with one. A dog is for life, not just for Xmas.

In the end we chose a handsome gun-dog with similar

colouring to Brandy of old. He was a long-legged spaniel with mercifully uncut tail. Madame told us that she thought he was around two years old. The vets gave them all a check-up on arrival, making notes on their condition and deducing their likely age from their teeth.

We had one or two questions. "What is his history? How did you come to get him in the first place?"

How did you come to fall in the water? I didn't come to fall in, I came to do some fishing...

"Shh!"

Madame replied that, as with many of their dogs, his history was unknown. With gun dogs it is sometimes the case that, for one reason or another, a dog fails to obey the master's commands or fails to do a good enough job in the field. She told us that it is quite common for people to abandon their dogs for a variety of reasons. She said that around one hundred thousand dogs are abandoned by their owners in France every year, many after the hunting season is over or at the start of the long summer holidays. She and her staff were always kept busy rounding up stray dogs, bringing them to the pound and ensuring they get checked over and tattooed in the ear. It is a requirement that all dogs in France must be tattooed with an identity number inside one of their ears (*tatouage*). This enables owners to quickly find their lost pets and it also prevents a vaccination certificate or similar from being used for more than one dog. She told us that our dog's identity number would be kept in a central computer, so that if we should subsequently lose our pet, we can contact her.

Looking around Madame's office we spotted several items that we would need immediately, so purchased from her a sturdy 'Rambo' lead — our dog looked pretty strong to me – plus two metal dishes for his food and water. After completing all the formalities, including our personal details which she immediately inputted onto the computer, I paid her the required seventy-five euros and led my companion to the car. The husband followed.

The dog stood on the pavement and despite several

'Hups' from us, refused to jump into the back of the car.

"Maybe he's bilingual?"

"Yes. Il n'ecoute ni en anglais ni en français!"

It was true. He didn't listen to us in either language. In the end we managed to hump him up and over the sill, nearly giving us both hernias into the bargain. The dog stood resolute and dignified in the back as we slammed the rear door down firmly, returned to our seats and accelerated away. Behind us retreated the upsetting whines of the unfortunate dogs we had to leave behind.

Back at home, the dog's new master took him on a tour of the premises, walking round and round in the hope that he (the dog) would perform. What we didn't realise, though, was that ever after, the dog would think that this would be his new job: parading round and round the house, like some sort of resident caretaker.

We named him Bruno.

Over the next few months we discovered that Bruno only liked to be outside. He remains intensely nervous of coming indoors, leading us to think that a previous owner might have enticed him inside and then slammed the door on him, imprisoning him for hours or days on end.

One sunny day Bruno and his master, or was it the other way round, went for a walk up the stony path around the back of our house to a very quiet country lane which runs in front of a large densely wooded copse. I had been used to taking Bruno off the lead, training him that I always had his favourite bits of cheese in my pocket, which he could have as long as he always returned to me instantly on command.

This particular day was the fist time that this manoeuvre would be attempted by Bruno and his master. The lead was duly unfastened and the dog went haring off, as usual, into the wooded copse. In due course, his master called him to heel. No response. After several calls and whistles, his master, not known for his phlegmatic temperament, began to get rather irate.

"Come here you little bugger."

Nothing.

Eventually, Bruno was spotted chasing a rabbit or some such and his master edged ever nearer, the trusty Rambo lead in his hands. Just when the task was almost completed, Bruno went haring off again, this time along the shady lane towards the farm fifty yards away. In the fields which border our property, the farmer's flock of woolly sheep and goats grazed peacefully, contentedly munching on their daily diet of grassy forage and hoary tree branches which were pulled down to their level by several intrepid goats.

"No, no Bruno. Come here," in increasing velocity. In response Bruno, with a wild, wall-eyed Marty Feldman look to his eyes, ducked his head underneath the farmer's electrified fence wire and galloped towards the grazing herds. In France, farmers are legally entitled to shoot any animal that endangers the lives of their flocks. Back at the house I had heard the commotion. I had been washing up in the kitchen which faces the distant back lane and with mounting alarm took in the scene unfolding directly in front of my horrified gaze. I dashed outside, frantically pulling on my garden shoes and chased up the lane.

By now, the farmer had rushed outside and was running towards Bruno who had by this time managed to do a rugby tackle on an unfortunate sheep, felling him heavily to the ground. By the time both men had arrived breathless on the scene, Bruno was busy biting one of the creature's back legs. The farmer and the dog's master between them managed to pull the now salivating dog off the poor sheep and Bruno's trusty lead was firmly clipped to his collar again.

"In France your dog must always have his lead on, always," said the irate farmer, even though we saw his own dog regularly wandering up and down the lane, clearly having to exercise himself. Anyway, at least that was what we understood of his statement. There seemed to be a few 'merdes' and other unfathomable words which our dictionary didn't for some reason contain.

Sheepish faces all round.

Thank God the farmer had not used his gun, but he looked none too pleased. What a start to my dreams of making friends with our new neighbours. That evening, the offending dog and his master in disgrace in the *sous-sol* (cellar), I collected our windfall of sweet plums from our garden and took a carrier-bag full around to the farmer's wife. I had noticed that in this southerly part of the world, the fruit crop is plentiful but ripens much earlier than in the UK. The farmer's wife was busy in her garden, evidently planting and weeding. I coughed to attract her attention, whilst leaning on her garden wall. She looked up.

"Je suis desolé pour mon mari et pour mon chien. Les deux sont maintenant dans le sous-sol."

The farmer's wife stared at me, incredulous. Surely I hadn't meant that the dog and his master had been sent in disgrace into the dark dungeon that was the *sous-sol*? She suddenly started laughing until tears streamed down her face. Her bony, liver-spotted fingers scrabbled in her apron pocket and hastily dabbed at her face with a well-scrubbed handkerchief. Another neighbour came over, an old lady of over eighty years, whose large whitewashed stone house was just discernible from our kitchen window. The farmer's wife gabbled something pretty incomprehensible to her, and she too laughed hysterically. Oh well. At least they hadn't shooed me off their land. So what if we have become the amusement spectacle of the region? I handed over my peace offering, and there were smiles all around. I told them as best I could that in future there would be no more running of the dog without a lead.

Quel catastrophe, mais c'est la vie!

15
Learning the lingo

H was looking frustrated. Despite several months of living here, no matter how hard he tried, he just couldn't understand what anyone was saying. I was always happy to translate, but as he said, what happens if I'm not around?

It's nice to feel needed, but clearly a solution was required.

For most people, studying French isn't such a handicap as it may appear at first, as long as you are aged below ten! The majority of children suddenly immersed in the language adapt quickly and most become reasonably fluent within three to six months, even though French schools make no concession whatsoever for foreign students, making no recourse to intensive courses, plunging all students (French or otherwise) straight into the pell-mell of school life. The only schools in France using English as the teaching language are a few international or foreign private schools.

But clearly the time for H to wear cap and short trousers and carry his books in a weighty leather satchel are long gone! We needed to look at adult classes and fast. It seems that if we want to make the most of the French way of life and enjoy to the full our time in France, it's essential to learn French as soon as possible. For people like us who have chosen to live in France permanently, learning French isn't just an option, it's a necessity. Although it isn't easy, we were told that even the most non-linguistic of people can soon acquire a working knowledge of the language. All that is required is a little hard work, application and some help and perseverance, particularly if we have only English-speaking colleagues and friends.

So, it was clearly *cherchez un cours français.* But, as I told H, this wasn't the time to get excited.

"Taking French classes doesn't mean a roomful of eagerly-attentive elderly men watching a girl dressed in black fishnet stockings slowly doing a striptease, au Moulin Rouge!"

He looked understandably disappointed.

So, we searched for a class that could accommodate an ageing geriatric with unfortunate memory-lapses. But enough of me, this was serious. At first we were pointed in the direction of a government-funded course that took place twice a week in nearby Villefranche de Rouergue. I say nearby, but this is France. It must have been at least fifty miles away.

The first day dawned and H set off for the school, armed with a clean writing pad, pen and simple French dictionary. After our habitual getting-lost stage, H arrived late and flustered and was directed to the beginner's (dunce's) seat.

Not a good start.

It wasn't helped by the fact that there were absolutely no English people in the class. He was surprised. The class seemed to be peopled almost entirely by Turkish and Armenian immigrants — somewhat off-putting for an elderly geriatric with English humour problems.

That evening, H had his head sunk in gloom.

"I can't go back there."

"Why not?" sympathetically.

"I didn't have the beginner's book I was supposed to have, and when during the lunch break I tried to buy it from where the teacher directed, the shop had never heard of it."

Something lateral was needed, and this turned out to be a week's intensive conversation classes at our nearby town, this time only fifteen kilometres away. This sounded much better for H. The course ran from nine to eleven each morning, then from one until three each afternoon. Of course, there was the standard two hour break for lunch in the middle of the day, but what did you expect. C'est la France, the land of *bien manger*.

Anyway, things certainly improved once H started

attending these, and I have to say it took some doing to persuade him to attend in the first place. But this time, he enjoyed himself much more. There were other elderly English geriatrics there, some believe it or not, with less French than H.

The girl who ran the courses was called Danielle. All conversation during the whole week was conducted solely in French. Absolutely no English was allowed, on pain of death, and they included all the subjects that might be encountered in normal daily life. There were classes on *la famille, chez le docteur, le corps humain, au restaurant* (but naturally), *rencontre avec le voisin* (meeting up with the neighbours) and *faire des commissions* (shopping).

After the first day, on hearing of all of this, I thought, great. That's exactly what H needs. He doesn't need to know yet the intricacies of all that difficult French grammar, just the kind of everyday phrases that will help him communicate here. I felt really relieved, until I heard that *comme d'habitude*, he had been trying to translate his English wordplay comedy routines into French.

"No, no. You can't do that," I cried.

"Why ever not. It'll make everyone laugh."

"Because...because...it just doesn't translate into French... I mean, the French use different kinds of phrases to us... You'll just have to take my word for it..." Exasperated.

The next night, I asked him how he had managed.

"Oh, O.K. We covered eating in a French restaurant today. I made everyone laugh."

"Oh no!" head in hands. "What did you say?"

"Well, Danielle was talking about wine and asked us to order a bottle as if we were sitting in a restaurant..."

"And...?" expecting the worst.

"Well, I can't understand why everyone laughed really. It sounded entirely reasonable to me. We did a little drama enaction, my colleague Bill acting as the waiter."

"Qu'est-ce que vous désirez, Monsieur? Nous avons un bon vin rouge ou un bon vin blanc," asked Bill in full waiter mode, asking whether I wanted red or white wine.

"Uh," not being absolutely sure, "Je voudrais un petit vin rouge et un petit vin blanc, les deux ensemble dans la verre, et voilà, il y a du vin rosé!"

"Oh no, you didn't?" I retorted incredulously. "The French would never, never, mix red wine with white to make rosé..."

But clearly, he had, because after that they broke up for lunch, his colleague Bill inviting him back to his house which was situated just yards from the centre. As Bill said: "It is clear that my friend is far too intoxicated to drive, so he'd better come home with me."

And so the week continued, each day bringing more bizarre accounts of his struggles with French wordplay routines. I dreaded the scenes following the doctor classes, but that seemed to pass off with relatively few problems, although I did wonder how H had learned the comparatively complicated word for bladder: *la vessie*. Better not to ask.

It was following the final day of the intensive course, the part that included a section on shopping, which was something I hadn't expected to cause any problems, that H returned in some annoyance.

"What's the matter?" I asked innocently. "Didn't it go well?"

"I don't see what was wrong with the suggestion that I made to Danielle."

"What did you say?" by now somewhat resigned to the inevitable.

"Well, I simply said that I saw no reason to learn the French names for the groceries. All we have to do is merely take along to the supermarket one item of what you require, hold it up to the assistant, and ask:

"Avez-vous quelque-chose comme ça?""

"No, no, no!" exasperated. "However can you expect to continue here in France if every time you need something, you take along something and ask the assistant: Have you got something like this? I mean, whatever will you do when you need a suppository?"

Enough said.

16
Renovations

The year was moving on. The intense heat of the summer was now mercifully tempered with a few cooling breezes, advertising the coming autumn. After telling all our neighbours about our plans for a new kitchen, it was time to put them to the test. We desperately wanted to find a local French builder to give us a *devis* quote to cement our credentials as a newly integrated family in the village, but that was where our troubles started. No-one wanted to know, even though the annual lengthy August break was now over. First we approached the large building company in the next village. Their advertising signs sprouted everywhere, from every hedgerow and bar. We called into their office, narrowly avoiding the assorted jumble of builders' trucks parked haphazardly in every direction, their sandy contents spilling uncompromisingly from every crevice of their tailgates.

At first we could find no-one, the office *un melange* of assorted papers, tools, filing cabinets and large black appointment books. Eventually a large, burly man bustled through, a stubby pencil behind his ear.

"Ah, nous cherchons un devis," hopefully.

"Comment?" apparently irritated by our interruption.

"Nous venons deménager à Paradis de Quercy et nous avons besoin d'une nouvelle cuisine." Just having moved to Paradis, we need a new kitchen, I repeated in my head.

As with most locals at first, he looked puzzled as he tried to make out my accented French, before finally cottoning on.

"Non. Ce n'est pas possible." We are a large company and we only take on complete house renovations. "Désolé."

We were disappointed.

"Well, can you recommend someone for us?"

"Sorry, no."

There was nothing for us to do but to return home and think again. Over the next few days we tried several other firms but all to no avail.

"Don't they want the business?" moaned H. Apparently not.

Several days later, by chance, we came to hear of an English self-taught builder who lived in one of the surrounding villages. He was a Londoner who had come to this neck of the woods, as did we, in search of a better life. But it soon became clear that he worked 'on the black' (*travail clandestine*), a practice as in most parts of the world which thrives in France, particularly amongst immigrant communities from outside the EU. It is illegal in France for non-EU nationals to work without a work permit, or for EU citizens to set up a business without a legitimate *siret* registered number.

Several French newspapers had made conservative estimates that the loss of tax revenue due to the 'black' or underground economy *(l'economie souterraine)* totals around five billion euros a year, with millions of people regularly doing *petit boulot* odd jobs for cash-in-hand payments. The newspapers often trumpet that up to thirty per cent of all work in France is not declared to the tax authorities. Of course there are numerous employers who deliberately make use of illegal labour so that they can get away with paying below the minimum wage, taking advantage also of exploiting long hours and poor working conditions into the bargain. We had heard that some locals get around the tax problems by agreeing with their workman to pay half in cash and half by *devis*. It all sounded far too complicated for me.

H and I contemplated what to do. On the one hand we had not been able to find a registered French builder who could take on the combined tasks of pulling down two internal walls and fitting our new kitchen, but neither were we happy about employing someone 'on the black' who would have no entitlement to social security benefits such as insurance against work injuries nor have insurance against faulty workmanship! We had also heard that, should the Maire hear that we had employed someone illegally, then it would be *us* who would be prosecuted — up to three years in some cases, as well as a hefty fine! There was also the fact that we didn't want to start our new village life by doing something that didn't feel right. If the work had merely entailed fitting the kitchen, we could have employed the fitters employed by a kitchen supplier, but it was the additional building work that was causing us extra headaches.

And then along came Jacques, a one-man French enterprise who came complete with his own siret number and, wonder of wonders, could commence the job in October. Because of the consequent disruption to life and limb, not to mention the dog, we decided to rent a villa in Biarritz for a month whilst the job was effected.

So, having suffered the inadequacies of no kitchen appliances for a couple of months we were ready and willing to start our unexpected holiday.

The leaves were already turning from green to bronze to gold on the oak trees fronting our lane when we packed the car full of our belongings and dog. As we opened the side windows, the heady fragrance of balsam permeated through from the five sinewy poplars in our back garden. So strong was the perfume that any signs of impending colds in the nose were instantly banished with just one heady whiff.

Our villa for the month was located in the town of Anglet, which nestles a stone's throw from the more famous Biarritz on the Atlantic coast. Anglet is a large commercial town in the Pyrenées Atlantique region of the Pays Basque, with two coastal *quartiers*, Chiberta and Chamberf d'Amour, each with amazingly long expanses of sandy surfing beaches. The villa suited our requirements down to the ground, having its own garden for Bruno to play in, and a forest opposite which comprised lovely walks through pine-covered paths, leading directly to the beach.

Despite the fact we were naturally concerned to know how Jacques was getting on having been left to his own devices in our home, everything went well for the first three weeks. We enjoyed our bracing walks every day, breathing in deeply the wonderful sea breezes which wafted and threaded their way to and fro across the open terrain. We ambled past the rambling eighteen hole Chiberta golf course, then turned along the narrow pedestrian walkway, fringed by low woody fence, which fronted the shingly sand dunes and famous spa centres, our faces permeated by the heady invigorating ozone.

One day as we kicked our bare heels through the white-tipped surf and Bruno barked at the incoming tides, we couldn't help but wonder at the well-trained French dogs that we met en route. Their owners did not hold fast to a Rambo lead, but let their dogs run, swim and play in the surf. "Why can't we let Bruno do that?" I asked innocently. Due to his past misadventures, H was somewhat sceptical.

But we let him off the lead anyway, having first let him sniff in my pocket for his favourite slivers of cheese rind that I always keep in the left pocket of my jogging trousers. With a yelp of joy and freedom, Bruno raced off along the promenade, his whispy tail aloft and acting as a rudder, his head held high with the sheer joy of it. Hand in hand, H and I walked behind him, momentarily content with our lives and enjoying the moment. But it would not last. We called him back.

"Bruno, Bruno….good boy….come here…."

But with that remembered wild Marty Feldman look, Bruno raced even further ahead, soon disappearing around a rocky promontory. I had just time to see the white tip of his tail as it disappeared up the wooden strutted walkway and into the golf course beyond.

Disaster!

Many hours later we sat shamefaced in the Anglet police station, explaining why we had disobeyed the law by walking a dog without a lead, by letting him foul the public highway and, horror of horrors, letting him scamper all around the Chiberta golf course whilst not having a membership card!

At the end of the week we returned to our home in Paradis in disgrace. But at least we had our brand-new kitchen to look forward to. After all, Jacques had been working hard for four weeks now so it should surely be finished. Amazingly we had a straight, clear drive home, not once taking the inevitable scenic route. We arrived home, tired and hungry, at six that evening. All the way home I had visions of my brand-new completed kitchen. We had plumped for units in real natural oak to complement our new solid oak table. I knew that wood units were considered rather old-hat in the UK at the moment but, because of our new enlarged salon layout, units that could double as items of salon furniture were required, rather than the clinical look of more modern white. I had also ordered vegetable wicker panniers, a carousel unit and inset oven, six-burner stainless-steel gas hob, inset dishwasher and a fridge-freezer which would have double doors hinged to one oak outer door, so that each time you opened the fridge door, the freezer door would remain shut to conserve the food.

I also couldn't wait to see our pièce de la résistance: a white stone pillar with inset old red bricks, plastered in an ancient rough, slightly wavy fashion to add character to the salon.

We crunched to a halt on our shingle drive and creaked open the doors. Bruno jumped out with a yelp of glee. He always yelps with abandon when going out with us, but then yelps with glee to come home again. Dogs. Who'd have 'em?

We pushed open the front door, noting that every light in the place was blazing, then stood there in shock and disappointment. The kitchen was nowhere near finished. In fact all that had been done was the knocking down of the two walls. Where were all our gleaming, brand new units and appliances, the ones I had so carefully chosen and agonised over? A heavy dust-sheet covered our salon furniture, a thick pall of brick dust and mortar hanging in mid-air swathes across the room, reminding me of the carcinogenic cigarette fog of my childhood home.

Jacques emerged from the gloom, a mortar trowel hanging

loosely in his right hand, the end of a disturbingly thin cigarette stub hanging loosely from his dry lips. The aroma from the cigarette did not smell like any kind of tobacco to me, but what did I know? I had led a very sheltered life.

"I didn't expect you back yet," Jacques said, or something to that effect.

"Obviously," said H. "How long will it take for you to finish the job?" hopefully.

"Bouff!" said Jacques.

Disappointed, tired and disgruntled, we trudged through the dustsheets, catching our feet inadvertently in the paint-spattered corners of tarpaulins as we lugged our suitcases through to the bedroom, which mercifully was still intact. All I wanted was to collapse on the bed and drown my sorrows in sleep.

Tomorrow was another day.

The following six weeks proved to be a nightmare of trying to live around a jobbing workman who would take three hours for his lunch every day and who kept asking for more money because of one problem or another. He kept pointing to his original *devis* which stated *"sans surprise."* I came to realise that this phrase encompassed any amount of increase in the price of the job that the builder could devise whilst on the job, so to speak. But slowly but surely our new kitchen began to take shape — literally around us. We became used to eating microwave meals, no doubt liberally sprinkled with brick dust, and spending a fortune on eating out, but *petit à petit* our kitchen was finally finished. I stood back and admired the finished article. There were the extra-deep pan drawers with specially silent gliding rails, over there the special, anti-scratch *nid* sink with its sliding glass vegetable board and sprinkler hose for all those healthy salads we planned to eat, and at last a stainless steel hob with six burners so that I could use several saucepans at one time without one handle tipping its neighbour over in messy confusion.

Merveilleuse!

Despite all our grumblings, Jacques had actually

completed the job. I couldn't believe it when we finally shook hands and said au revoir to him. At last our house was our own again. Now we could in truth *bien manger* to our heart's content, in our very own kitchen with not a dust-sheet, tarpaulin or exotic cigarette in sight.

Thank God.

17
Essential requirements

"I can't live without a TV," said he. "How can I live without watching Eastenders?"

"Oh, all right," resignedly. What was the point in moving to France if all we were going to do was watch Eastenders? But I had to admit, he did have a point. It was now March in France, and although feeling lyrical, *"It is the first mild day of March, each minute sweeter than before, the redbreast sings from the tall larch that stands beside our door,"* Wordsworth didn't have him indoors to contend with.

All those months ago when we were contemplating the move, if I'd made a wish list it would have been to own a dream home in the sunshine but still have our favourite bits from the UK: TV and Radio 4. An additional bonus would be that we could improve our French by listening to the local French channels. Maybe we could have it all, after all.

So we made the long trip to LeClerc in Montauban and didn't need much persuasion or French to enable the salesman to sell us a large, widescreen TV – well, our eyes might become more longsighted as we get older. That was our excuse anyway. We also took the opportunity to buy some French plugs. (No, not sink plugs, nor rawl plugs, nor advertising plugs.....). We were fed up with having to use those awkward English plug adaptors every time we needed to switch something on.

Even for us it proved very straight-forward to wire on French plugs to our old UK appliances. They sell two types of plug here, two or three pin. If our appliance has two wires, we need to use the two pin, if three wires, then it is essential that we use a three pin plug in order to provide an earth connection. It seems that the French do not distinguish between live or neutral so on a two pin plug it does not matter which way we connect the wires. On a three pin plug, the earth wire is yellow/green on both UK and French appliances and that wire needs connecting to the centre connection (the female pin on the plug), the other two wires to the other pins. The main difference is that French plugs don't have fuses. So, no more worries over whether you need a thirteen, five or three amp. Customers back in England never did seem to know which fuse to use, usually irrationally plumping for the largest ampage, thinking that that should cover all purposes. Wrong! But here in France plugs don't use a fuse at all. That solves that then. If all this sounds confusing, it is still safer to rewire than use our UK adaptors, especially for high wattage appliances like heaters for his ageing bones and kettles for my constant cups of tea. It does help, though, if you know how to wire a UK plug or have basic knowledge of wires inside plugs. Him indoors did from his many years losing money in the DIY trade and helping customers who had bought their products elsewhere!

Now that we are *au fait* with the plugs, we turned our attention to our new, super-dooper flat-screen TV. Our first question was of course: how can we actually obtain English TV programmes in France? I'd heard that it is illegal to watch Sky in France, but was this true? We asked around. Apparently the whole subject is a grey area. Sky's broadcasting licence covers only the UK. However, BBC and some other channels are available in unencrypted format via satellite so it can be argued that they are thus freely available to anyone. Because of Sky's licensing restriction, though, you can't subscribe to any Sky service from a foreign address, you shouldn't connect the Sky box to a telephone line if it's overseas (which means you can't use most of the interactive services) and you should never phone Sky from overseas. The best and only way to connect to Sky is from a UK address or via the numerous companies that will supply and instal Sky systems overseas. We therefore chose the latter. We thought this would be O.K. because if it were illegal then these companies would surely not be allowed to operate so openly.

Voilà! It's working. We can now watch BBC1, 2, 3, 4 plus News 24, ITV, Film4 etc. etc. But we have discovered, during a recent thunderstorm, that if it rains we get pixelated faces on all the actors, and a steadily increasing 'chunking' sound, that's really quite alarming. There have been many instances when we've just reached the dénôument in a particularly exciting film only to have to switch the set off because it started to rain outside! Oh, the wonders of modern technology.

But, at least I can now get my daily fix of Radio 4. We've had workmen fix two large *paraboles* on the roof, one for French and one for English programmes. Apparently the further south you are, the bigger the dish has to be, so we weren't taking any chances.

However, after a while I began to recognise that we needed more immersion in the real French language, so, with the aid of our separate handset (all these gadgets are getting to me, bit by bit) I switched channels. France has six terrestrial stations broadcasting throughout the country. There's France 2 and France 3, which are both state-owned and operated by French Télévision, and TF1. These are all free to air, but with the inevitable French adverts. They're quite amusing, really, especially the adverts we were familiar with back in the UK, with the same actors now lip-synching in perfect French.

Franck told me that the public channels in France aren't permitted to raise more than twenty-five percent of their revenue from advertising. Limits are imposed on the amount of TV advertising, which may not average more than six minutes per hour per day, with a maximum of twelve minutes in any single hour. I'm sure we received more than this in the UK.

Now that we can switch from watching English news programmes to those on France's TF1 station, it has slowly dawned on us why we feel more satisfied with French news. There is a world of difference in how the media portrays it and we were in an ideal position to note the differences and effects on us. I had always thought that the public in the UK is manipulated by the media in what it chooses to present to us all. And here was all the evidence I needed. The English news channels are dominated by sometimes only two main stories — consistently Iraq and Afghanistan – often to the exclusion of all else that must be happening in the world, but particularly in the different regions of the UK. Apart from sport, there is nothing to lighten the viewer's load at all.

In direct contrast, the French news channels trawl across the different départements, giving a balanced look at what is happening across the country — sometimes lightweight, yes, but it doesn't matter. Often there will be a report on how the champagne industry is faring or reports on other European cities like Venice with its incumbent watery problems or those of the leaning tower at Pisa. Yes, the French channels do include world events, but these do not saturate the news to the exclusion of all else. We have therefore decided, in an attempt to cure my depression, no longer to watch English news. Anything important happening in the UK will still be available on the French channels.

A TV licence (*rédevance sur les postes de télévision*) is required by most TV owners in France, costing currently one hundred and sixteen euros, fifty a year for a colour set. The licence fee covers any number of TVs (owned or rented), irrespective of where they're located in France. For instance, you might want to instal one in a holiday home, in a motorised vehicle or even in a boat, although the government is considering levying the licence on each set. Apparently, though, even if you bring a UK set to France and intend only using it to watch videos, you must still have a valid licence.

If you buy a TV in France like us, the old rule was that a retailer was obliged to inform the relevant authority so that a licence fee bill would follow automatically after a few months. This, not surprisingly, led to many French people paying upfront in cash and then giving a fictitious address. However, what we have now discovered is that our first *taxe d'habitation* (residence tax) bill will include as standard the licence fee, making it far more difficult to dodge paying it.

Damn!

It's called inertia selling ("invented by a Scotsman," says H – 'in Ayrshire'), forcing the few who don't possess a TV to actively claim back the licence fee tax. The other main tax we will shortly need to pay is the property tax or *taxe foncière*.

"Does that mean I only have to pay it 'once a year' (fonce a year)?"

"Grrr."

I have now taken to watching the daily *met*éo weather forecasts, followed by the main evening news programmes on the French channels. They start at around eight o'clock and last half an hour. I must admit that a certain dishy *Patrick* or even the gorgeous *Harry* who regularly read the news are no reason why I watch the French news so avidly! Often the news and *met*éo programmes are followed by a film. I was amused to hear, though, that French TV channels aren't allowed to show films on Friday or Saturday nights, as this is deemed 'unfair' competition to the cinemas!

In our nearest large town, there is a wonderful cinema called *Le Querlys*. No, I don't know why it's called such a strange name, but it is a wonderfully warm, intimate place, just like the old Gaumont I used to attend as a child. In our local Boulangerie, each month *La Boulangère* offers a free programme of forthcoming films at *Le Querlys*, both in English and in French, so we always know what's on.

We watched a wonderful film last month called *La Môme* (the kid). As I write this, it is shortly to be filmed in the UK under its English title *La vie en rose*. But there's something about watching a French film in its original version where you catch that indefinable *je ne sais quoi* and *joie de vivre*, which can be lost somewhat in translation. Certainly the young French actress who played the wonderful singer Edith Piaf was sensational. Near the end of the film I caught him indoors, of the stoical and unemotional manner, quite close to needing a tissue. Certainly, afterwards he was to be found heading for the nearest bar for a stiff drink of whisky. Well, any opportunity that affords itself….

Rubbish

H had noticed that there were no black dustbins conveniently placed outside our back door, as in the UK. We were certainly noticing how different life was in the country versus our industrial urban town back home. I had noticed the three large rubbish containers at the top of our lane, of course up-hill. What else would you expect? So, it was clear that we would need to regularly transport all our large black sacks of household rubbish up the hill and deposit them in the relevant container.

Our monthly village bulletin from the Mairie tells us that household rubbish is collected once a week in our area. We are all expected to separate our rubbish into various bags so that they can be recycled.

Not wanting to do the wrong thing, I cautioned H (who was likely to be the one doing all the carrying) to make sure he always put our bags into the correct recycling bin. But, as usual, he had an argument against this.

"Don't see the point," said he.

"Why not?" innocently.

"Saw the rubbish removals truck last week. The men jumped out and smartly cleared all three containers of their contents and dumped the lot wholesale into the back of their truck."

"No!"

"Oh yes," smirking.

So, what was the point of all this recycling message, then? To some things there are no answers.

As far as other, more personal, forms of waste are concerned it seemed that although properties in urban areas are normally connected to mains drainage (*tout à l'égout*), as we were living in a rural area, we had to make do with a *fosse toutes eaux* (also known as a *puits* perdu, or lost well) buried within our own grounds.

"How are we supposed to know when it's full?" said H,

picturing the scene.

"God only knows. Let's hope it's not a rude awakening one morning."

Franck told me, after a suitably careful question, that our *fosse toutes eaux* takes all our waste water except rainwater. Some older *fosses toutes eaux* apparently have an aerator (*brouilleur* or *batteur*) to help break down the solid matter and allow it to settle while clear water overflows into an underground drainage system.

I discovered that it is necessary to check the small-print when purchasing all cleaning materials and toilet bleaches that they are *convient pour fosses septiques* because otherwise they would not break down properly during the process. This was also necessary with toilet paper, so I now had a ready-made excuse why we could no longer buy that expensive, thick, loo paper that was constantly being advertised on TV.

"What a load of rubbish," said H.

18
It all makes work for the working man to do

THE GASMAN COMETH

'Twas on the Monday morning, the Gas man came to call.
The gas tap wouldn't turn - I wasn't getting gas at all.
He tore out all the skirting boards to try and find the main,
And I had to call the carpenter to put them back again.
Oh, it all makes work for the working men to do.

'Twas on the Tuesday morning. the Carpenter came round.
He hammered, and he chiselled, and he said, "Look what I've found:
Your joists are full of dry rot, but I'll put them all to rights."
Then he nailed right through a cable and out went all the lights.
Oh, it all makes work for the working men to do.

'Twas on the Wednesday morning the Electrician came.
He called me 'Mister Sanderson', which isn't quite my name.
He couldn't reach the fuse box without standing on the bin,
And his boot went thru a window, so I called a glazier in.
Oh, it all makes work for the working men to do.

'Twas on the Thursday morning the Glazier came along,
With his blowtorch and his putty and his merry glazier song.
He put another pane in - it took no time at all -
Then I had to get a painter in to come and paint the wall.
Oh, it all makes work for the working men to do.

'Twas on the Friday morning the Painter made a start.
With undercoats, and overcoats, he painted every part,
Every nook and cranny, but I found when he had gone
He'd painted over the gas tap, and I couldn't turn it on!
Oh, it all makes work for the working men to do.

On Saturday and Sunday they do no work at all,
So it was on the Monday morning that the Gas man came to call.

Flanders and Swann

It was a Monday morning in August in Paradis and the sun was blazing down. The earth all around our plot had been baked so hard that cracks were widening in crazy, zig-zag patterns in the red clay surrounding our house. My other half was peering solemnly into one particularly large crack, aimlessly tracking the route of an army of red ants who were busily running hither and thither, into and out again, totally engrossed in their ant business.

"Looking down this crevasse reminds me of that trip we made over the Grand Canyon for our Pearl wedding, remember?" said he.

"What? Be serious for a minute. D'you think we should do anything?" suddenly worried, as per usual.

"Maybe we should look in our new insurance policy...... what's French for subsidence?"

"Subsidence is a French word."

"Oh. But I wouldn't like to tackle a French conversation about it."

"No. Me neither..."

"I wonder why we took out the policy, then?"

Seemed like yet another problem to be filed in my personal, ever-lengthening 'DB' file. "What's DB?" you might ask. Disbuggerment. Whenever I come across an apparently unsolvable situation, or something about which I can't quite make up my mind, I file it subconsciously into my DB file and soon, voilà, it seems to sort itself out, one way or another.

That settled, we wandered around the house to our large front garden and surveyed the scene. The lawn, or rather the couch-grass, had been burnt to just the same sienna shade as that of our neighbours, so there clearly wasn't much point in attempting to cut it. However, there was one section which looked different from the rest. We wandered down to take a closer look. In amongst the seered sections, a long bright-green swathe of springy turf had established itself. It appeared to run down, more or less in a straight line, from the house to the lane which fronted our property. He who likes to ponder over these things eventually pronounced the existence of water underground, but he was puzzled.

"Can't be a natural spring."

"Why not?"

"It's too straight. Naturally flowing water tends to meander, but this green swathe of grass is dead-straight."

I decided to ask our local Mairie to send a man to investigate, then settled down to wait the requisite six months. Nothing happens fast in France. So, we were very surprised that very afternoon to be jolted out of our afternoon siesta by the arrival of two workmen in the standard Citroën Berlingo ubiquitous to this region. Every farmer, agriculturalist, gardener, workman etc. seems to drive one. I later gathered that car insurance companies here charge less for French vehicles. What a good idea. I wondered why the UK didn't follow suit. It would do wonders for Longbridge and all those other UK car-manufacturers currently suffering from too much global competition.

Anyway, we shook hands with the two workmen as they surveyed the scene. One scratched his bulbous nose whilst the other issued an exclamation.

"Bien sûr, c'est le tuyeau (water pipe)," said Jean-Pierre, the rotund friendly one.

"What's wrong with it?" innocently.

"Split." He made a funnel shape with his hands and pursed

his lips in a swishing sound. "No good," he repeated in his best schoolboy English.

"Does the Mairie cover such work?" hopefully.

"Non. La faute, c'est à votre côté." On our side of the water meter, naturally! "Donc, c'est à vous à payer." It is therefore your responsibility to pay, naturally!

"How much?" said him indoors.

"Bouff," said both workmen in unison.

Him indoors and me had a quick conference. Neither of us knew for certain how long the water might have been gushing out of the evidently underground inlet pipe, but we knew that the longer it went on, the higher would be our water bill at the end of the year.

"OK," I said in frustration. "When can you start?"

"Oh no," they replied. "We can't do it. You should call M. Bertrand. He is the only one with the mini-pelle machine to dig the trench."

We knew the name Bertrand. He was the son-in-law of the man who had originally sold us the house. My heart sank. Yet more difficult French to conjure up, trying to explain the intricacies of work that I didn't really understand myself. "Can you call him for us?" I said hopefully to Jean-Pierre.

"Oui, bien sûr."

They went away whilst him indoors went to find his calculator.

Several days later a large machine suddenly appeared, crunching up our gravel drive, its wildly-flailing bucket at the front narrowly missing our best flower borders. I rushed out to try and save Bruno from becoming ground into bonemeal beneath its heavy wheels, but the dog must have sensed the imminent danger as I found him later cowering in our underground sous-sol. It was his favourite retreat, a place where he always went when confused and uncertain. I thought that one of these days I might join him.

M. Bertrand surveyed the scene. "Bouff!" he said.

"How much?" said him indoors.

"Huit cents."

"I'll pay you seven hundred and no more." He can be so

masterful on occasions.

Much scratching of M. Bertrand's beard whilst he contemplated this. "My machine she is very expensive," he remonstrated.

"My wife, she is also very expensive," came the quick retort.

A pregnant silence ensured, until M. Bertrand finally agreed to this ludicrously cheap piece of labour. He jumped back up onto his mini-pelle and, manoeuvring it into position at the one end of the broad swathe, he began to dig a broad wide trench right through our previously beautiful front garden. Either side, great mountains of red clay steadily grew as he grunted and chortled his way through the deep terrain. As the trench was finally dug, as if by magic who should turn up but Jean-Pierre and his mate. Handshakes and much hearty greeting between the three Frenchmen as they gabbled and 'bouffed' their way through the intricacies of the job in hand. Apparently then satisfied, Jean-Pierre and mate then disappeared from whence they had come whilst M. Bertrand proceeded to fit the replacement length of pipe. Once complete, he then jumped back on his machine and proceeded, with some dexterity it must be said, to replace the mounds from either side into the centre ground again, up the length of the disturbed terrain.

After several hours, when the noise had finally stopped, I asked M. Bertrand how we could be sure that this new pipe wouldn't fracture also. He reassured me by saying that the old pipe was very old, and this new pipe was much stronger, specially constructed to survive the perils of animals or the invasion of tree roots. There was nothing we could do but pay the man, albeit with heavy hearts, and bid him a good day.

The following day, as luck would have it, we noticed that our phone wasn't working. We had no dial tone, nor any tonality on any of the buttons. Thankfully I had already endured the rigors of buying a mobile phone from France Télécom, so now phoned them to try to explain the problem with our fixed line. I had learned the hard way that it is no good people like us buying a 'pay as you go' mobile phone deal, as at the end of every three months any unused amounts of credit are declared null and void. For our essentially emergencies-only requirements, we eventually found a cheap seven euros a month deal which suited our purposes much better. But we had had to learn the hard way, as usual.

But now facing the current situation and having got through to France Telecom, I was regaled with the infuriating introductory melodies endured by all callers before having to listen carefully to the recorded message in very fast French. "If you want this, *tappez un*; if you want that, *tappez deux*...." and so on, followed by: "and to finish *tappez dieze* (which I think means the hash sign)." The whole process is infuriating enough in England, let alone in another language. Eventually, after many attempts and much futile hanging around, I managed to attract the attention of a real person. I quickly explained the problem in my halting French and he promised to send a man around.

'Twas on the Wednesday morning that the man from France Télécom duly arrived. He ummed and ahhed, much like others of his compatriots, before finally pronouncing that the phone wire under the ground was broken. It was necessary to dig a trench to lay a new *fil* and *gaine* (conduit) underground.

"But, we have just had a trench dug there to repair our water pipe…"

"*Ah, voilà, c'était ça,*" said France Télécom. "It is undoubtedly that that has caused the problem. There should always be a *gaine* conduit to protect the wire when fitted underground."

This was getting ridiculous. In desperation, I gave the phone man my mobile and asked him to telephone M. Bertrand to argue over how to resolve the problem. It was obvious, surely, that M. Bertrand had cut through the wire whilst replacing the water pipe so therefore must surely agree to pay for the problem. The irony was that, as the son-in-law of our vendor, it was probably he who had put in the original phone wire (without the *gaine*) in the first place!

Soon, much gabbled expensive talking on *my* mobile ensued, before I was informed that M. Bertrand would return but that he denied it was his fault. We told him to get back here pronto. In the meantime the man from France Télécom connected a temporary *provisoire* phone wire, laying it loosely and haphazardly right the way down our front lawn and asked us to sign his chitty.

"But, does this mean that I have to pay you? I thought that this sort of thing was covered by the rental I pay on the fixed line," stupidly.

"La problème, ce n'était pas la faute du Télécom," he blithely informed us. *Of course not*. "C'est à vous à payer." The problem is not the fault of Telecom…it is you who must pay! So, if madame could please sign his chitty, he would be on his way.

More frustration.

Three days later we heard the now familiar grunting and chuntering of M. Bertrand's mini-pelle as it wended its crunching way up our gravel drive. We no longer had to worry about Bruno. The instant he heard the sound, he was off to his retreat.

"Now, see here M. Bertrand," said him indoors. "It's obvious that you must have cut through our phone wire when you repaired the water pipe. So, you must agree that it is entirely feasible that you dig this new trench entirely at your own expense."

"Non! Ce n'était pas ma faute," said he. *Of course not*. "C'était parce-que l'ancien était trop vieux. Donc, c'est à vous à payer." It is not my fault…It is because the old wire was too old…Therefore it is you who must pay." *This is becoming a farce…where's Brian Rix?*

"It's you who's too old," muttered my other half underneath his breath. "But, why didn't you fit un gaine on the old wire originally?"

"Ah, en cette epoque-là, elle n'existe pas." In that epoch such a conduit didn't exist in France.

I wish you didn't exist, thought he.

The two men continued to argue, one in perfect French, the other in some sort of childish Franglais. We were realising how difficult it is to complain and argue in another language. But the Frenchman would not budge. Either we paid him upfront, or he refused to do the work. Eventually, we agreed to pay him a lesser sum, albeit in considerable annoyance. He then proceeded to dig exactly the same trench as before, throwing exactly the same red clay mountains either side of the deepening rift before replacing them *au centre*, as before.

We could only hope and pray that he wouldn't fracture anew the brand new water pipe....

All the while Bruno watched from the sous-sol, ever puzzled over the stupidities of man. *When I bury my bone, I don't then proceed to dig it up again and re-bury it ad infinitum....*

As our bank balance becomes ever smaller, it all makes work for the working man to do.

19
Un anniversaire

It's December in Paradis and the frost is lying hard and crunchy underfoot.

"Thought this was supposed to be the south of France," said he, grumbling as usual, as he rummaged in his drawers for his drawers.

I must admit it has taken us quite by surprise how cold it gets here in the winter. It's a different kind of cold, though, from the UK. The skies are often royal blue, the kind you get in Switzerland. But you would never get him indoors to go skiing: not good for the ageing bones.

It was while we were out for a bracing walk that I realised next month was a rather important milestone: his sixtieth birthday. What should I do? This wasn't the place to buy humorous birthday cards, however appropriate. All that the local shops seemed to have were strange cards that, when you reached home and opened the cellophane, you realised didn't open at all. I contemplated it for a while, thinking all the while that such a card was really very appropriate. It was just like him: he never does what he's supposed to do either! However, it is a big occasion so over the next few days I racked my brains on what I could do to mark the day.

The following day I discovered a leaflet which someone had rammed into our postbox. All properties around here have dark-green post boxes fixed to their front walls. Each day Madame La Poste arrives in her smart yellow Renault Clio and, with her special key, crams all the unwanted advertising rubbish into our very own box. Sometimes, hiding beneath all this stuff is an important envelope from the Tax Office or suchlike.

I ran down the fifty yards(!) to our postbox and turned the key. The usual unsolicited rubbish. Anyway I had almost thrown the stack of paper away into our brand-new stainless steel kitchen bin – the one I call Arkwright because however careful you are, the lid always snaps onto your fingers at the last minute - when I espied a yellow leaflet advertising a special Fête which was happening in our village's Salle des Fêtes on the very day of his birthday. I retrieved my French:English dictionary and ploughed through the details. All the inhabitants of our village had been invited to a grand *repas* with music and dancing. I glanced down the menu.

Repas de champêtre
Apéritif
Petite salade de tomates
Saumon fume d'Ecosse
Délice de l'Escargot de Bourgogne
Les poissons du jour
Dessert ou des fromages
Vin
Café compris
Prix: 17Euros. Enfants de 10 ans: 9Euros

Although the food wasn't exactly our cup of tea, it was the right day so I tried furtively to get my other half's interest.

"Look, dear, there's a party happening in the village on the 17th."

He glanced sceptically down the menu. "Can't eat snails…"

"I know, dear, but you know what these French do's are like. There are so many courses that if you don't like something, just eat some bread, wait awhile, and something else soon comes round – rather like life really. It would be nice, wouldn't it, to go out on your birthday?"

"Bloody hell. What day is it?"

"You know very well."

He knew he was about to lose the argument, so grumblingly agreed. His eye flicked to the price. "How much? P'raps I should go in short trousers…"

Typical.

My mind was frantically working at something. The next day I was at our local Boulangerie. We are fortunate that it has an Artisan sign outside, proclaiming to all that fresh bread is baked right there on the premises. As if the delicious smells emanating from the vicinity were not sufficient inducement in themselves. And the pâtisserie... How ever am I supposed to lose weight?

Anyway, I took the opportunity to ask Madame La Boulangère: "*Est-ce que vous pouvez faire cuire au four un gateau special pour l'anniversaire de mon mari?*"

"*Oui. Bien sûr.*"

She asked me his name and age. I told her but said that one candle would be enough. You know when you're getting old, when the candles cost more than the cake! I told her to be sure to keep the cake a secret as it was a surprise, and arranged for her to deliver it directly to the Salle des Fêtes on the 17th.

The big day arrived, cold but bright, and we prepared to leave for the party. We had wondered what to do with Bruno, as always. Our grounds were now pretty-well fenced all around, with a secure gate, so we thought this would be a good opportunity to see how he would fare if we left him on his own in the garden. Most times when we went out we took the car and he always travelled with us in the back, but this time we were only going round the corner in the village so intended to go on foot.

We crunched down the gravel drive, gingerly feeling our way amongst the icy runnels. Bruno, as usual, was excitedly running up and down the garden, barking frantically at the sheep in the field next-door, and the sheep as usual ignored him, continuing to graze contentedly without a murmur, *comme d'habitude*. Once we reached the gate, we sidled quickly through and as calmly as we could, we waved goodbye to Bruno.

"See you soon, Bruno. We won't be long. Look after the place for us, won't you? There's a good boy," hopefully.

He stood disconsolately at the gate, not believing his eyes

as we shut the gate firmly on his golden snout. We marched confidently along the lane, trying not to look back. A few plaintive yelps followed us, but we were determined that we weren't going to give in to him. He had to learn that we couldn't always take him with us.

At the corner of the lane, we crossed what serves as the main road in the village and walked the hundred yards to the Salle des Fêtes. Even if we hadn't known where it was, the lilting strains of an accordion would have guided us. It was clear we were going to be regaled with all the latest tunes, if this one was anything to go by. We certainly recognised "Oh my Papa," followed by "Under the bridges of Paris with you," whatever it was called, and then 'She' by Charles 'As-no-voice.

We walked in. I braced myself for the inevitable three kisses by all the elderly gentlemen of the village, trying not to clash glasses or noses in the process. Always difficult to know which cheek you are supposed to proffer first.

"Bonjour, monsieur. Bonjour, madame," even if we hadn't a clue who any of these people were. The usual group of English were standing in a corner. Every time we met we all agreed with one another that we shouldn't form la clique anglaise, but every time we were inevitably drawn to one another. For all our love for this part of the world, it was such a relief to be able to converse in adult conversations instead of the usual French schoolboy phrases we had managed to master.

It must have been half an hour later when the meal was about to be served that a late-comer whispered to me:

"I'm sure I just saw Bruno outside the Boulangerie."

"No," I replied confidently. "Can't be. We left him securely in the garden. He can't get out."

"Well," she said. "It certainly looked like him. I can't think of another dog in the village who looks like that with a red collar."

My heart sank. "Oh no."

Quick as a flash, my other half said he would go and take a look. Before I could say anything, he was gone.

Oh no. What about the cake? It might be brought in at any moment, and he wouldn't be here!

There was nothing I could do but save him a place, bite my fingernails, and hope for the best. The first course was brought in, and the accordionist commenced his main repertoire to much cheering.

No sign of him indoors. I saved his full plate from being collected up and resigned myself. *Que sera sera.*

After about thirty minutes, at last the wanderer returned.

"Where've you been?" I asked. "I've got your first two courses here, which I've shoved into the centre of the table. What happened?"

"It *was* Bruno! He must have jumped the fence. Madame la Boulangère gave me a rope and I managed to catch him and drag him home."

"But where is he now?"

"In the car, the other end of the village. Looking for a parking space round here today was like the last time I went to a football match back home…."

I heaved a huge sigh of relief. At least the dog was safe, my other half was here and nothing yet had happened. He just had time to gulp down the apéritif (with his pair of teeth) and the salade before the organiser of the fête walked up to the microphone on the stage. She thumped the mike several times — making me think of Norman Collier in those old northern stand-up comic series on TV - in a desperate bid to institute some measure of calm in the proceedings. Still the diners wouldn't stop their conversations. She banged the mike more loudly before, eventually, amidst many "Shushes" or the French equivalent, silence at last reigned around the room.

"Mesdames, messieurs. Aujourd'hui il y a un grande surprise pour le monsieur qui est assis là-bas."

She clapped her hands and nodded to the kitchen at the back of the room. A door opened and a lady emerged, bearing aloft an enormous iced fruit cake with single candle glowing.

"*C'est l'anniversaire soixante,*" the microphone boomed, much to my other half's chagrin. He had been eyeing up the blonde lady to his left and now she and everyone else knew exactly how old he was. *Quel domage*.

All heads craned towards our table, where my other half in some confusion was kissed on both cheeks by the lady bearing the cake, almost dropping the whole plate down her large cleavage during her exertions. He was then instructed to suck in his cheeks in order to blow out the one candle *au centre*. He did as he was told, to much illogical applause and patting on the back. He stood up and bowed, to more applause, before sitting down to much discomforture.

And the accordionist, in broken English, sang: "Happy birthday to you…" followed by the French version, which surprisingly was very much the same, if a little bit of a tongue twister: "*Bon anniversaire à vous, bon anniversaire à vous…*"

The meal resumed and our red cheeks cooled a little. He looked around the room, spotting a large grey-haired gentleman sitting over in the corner.

"Is that *Monsieur le Maire* sitting over there?" he whispered.

"Yes."

"I think we should send him a slice of cake."

"That's a nice idea, but why?"

"I haven't paid our water bill."

20
Our first visitors

Our son and daughter, complete with American son-in-law, are coming over in the summer. Help! Although we have now been in France for nearly two years, they will be our first summer visitors. It's kind of a celebratory year really because not only will we celebrate our Ruby anniversary, I will reach that dreaded pensioner age of sixty later in the year.

As we have six months' notice of their visit, we have decided to instal our very own swimming pool. Out here it is not classed as a luxury, but a necessity. Of course him indoors looked at the costs and I read all the glossy brochures. We contrasted the various costs against the undoubted health benefits which swimming every day in salt water would give us, especially with his leg. We decided to go ahead.

I contacted various pool shops and eventually plumped for the one with the lady who spoke English! Well, it's so much easier when you can explain exactly what you want. She tried to sell us a luxurious in-ground pool at forty-thousand euros, but we felt that as we weren't planning on registering for an Olympic event just yet, nor on scooping the top prize in the Euro Lottery (more's the pity), we would plump for the cheaper option of an above-ground version. She told us that we could have it installed *demi-enterré*, half in the ground and half out.

"But," asked him indoors, "haven't we got to have those expensive security fences and alarms with that?"

A recent French law, completely illogically, decrees that all in-ground pools must have security barriers and alarms in case a small child falls in. I say illogically because you don't need such measures if you have a deep pond in your back garden, which drowns you just as dead as any pool will.

She responded: "No. You do if it's a completely in-ground pool, but because yours will have a small wall around it, you won't need to." We also felt it was a good choice in that Bruno was less likely to be able to take a midnight swim and then be unable to get out again.

That settled it. With growing excitement we ordered our very first pool and felt like Lord and Lady Muck. We told the shop that it *must* be installed before the end of July when our visitors were due to arrive.

"No problem," she said, ushering us out of the shop.

I should have realised. Nothing, and I mean nothing, moves fast in France.

Springtime came and went and still no pool. I rang the shop several times, but the lady said that the problem was the extremely wet conditions we had unusually been having. She apologised but said that the *mini-pelle* digging machine couldn't travel over our garden in the wet. The heavy clay would create deep ridges all over the place and make the digging and drainage difficult. With heavy heart, I settled down to wait some more.

It rained all over June but eventually July arrived with blazing sunshine. Thank God. The men duly arrived and I asked them:

"Where is our pool?"

"Un camion va arriver à tout à l'heure."

They set about marking out the terrain with chalk and string, and I wondered how long we would be left with this large hole in the garden. Him indoors said he was looking into it. But soon enough a lorry arrived and unloaded several heavy boxes. We blithely signed, hoping we weren't signing our lives away. The men set to work, first levelling the ground somehow (it was on a sharp incline), then cementing the base, then fixing the many rigid supports before unrolling the resin walls of our new pool. In the meantime they set about installing the sand and salt filtration systems in our nearby barn, connecting the hoses through the brick wall.

"Voilà," they said in unison when all was ready.

We set about with our hose-pipe. We asked the men how long it would take to fill, as it was a large pool, 9m by 4.5 m. Sounded like one of those dreadful school arithmetic questions that I never could solve. They scratched their prickly chins and agreed it should only take about six hours.

"That's all right then," I thought, noting to myself that the family was due to arrive in four days.

Three days later and the pool still wasn't full! Apparently we had a small bore (yes, I know), so the whole operation was very slow. On the morning of the visit, we checked the pool and, thank God, it was now full. Just in the nick of time, we dosed it with the large bag of salt we had purchased from the *Intermarché* hypermarket in the nearby large town and switched on the filtration pump.

The family have at last arrived! The sun is shining and we're having a great time. Despite the fact that both our children are vegetarian, and French restaurants do not appear to understand the concept, we are managing to eat very well. I had prepared in advance loads of vegetarian lasagne just in case (no, just in the freezer) — well, I am a worrier — but so far all has gone according to plan. Franck, our neighbour, on hearing that our children ate neither meet nor fish (in fact, nothing with a face, as our daughter so accurately evinced), took just one phrase to describe the scenario: "c'est un catastrophe!" But then he is French, the race that will eat absolutely anything that breathes and moves, in as little time as it takes to cover it in sauce.

As our daughter and son-in-law saw a TV programme in the US about the nearby Millau Viaduct, they both evinced a desire to go and see it in person. *Le Viaduc de Millau* is a large cable-stayed road-bridge that spans the valley of the river Tarn near Millau in the south-west of France. One of its designers was actually an English architect by the name of Norman Foster, and the bridge itself is billed as being the tallest vehicular bridge in the world, taller than the Eiffel

Tower and only just shorter than the Empire State Building in New York.

"This I must see," said our son-in-law. "The guy on the TV program said that this Millau bridge is now the highest road bridge deck in the world and that only the bridge deck of the Royal Gorge Bridge in Colorada, but that's mainly a pedestrian bridge over the Arkansas River, is considered the highest bridge in the world."

As a former G.I. and with that look in his eye, who was I to refuse?

As H and I had never visited it before either, I dusted off our much-thumbed local road-map and we pored over it to plot a route. We saw that the viaduct is actually part of the main A75-A71 autoroute in the Département of Aveyron, which runs directly from Paris to Béziers. Apparently, before 2004 when the bridge was first constructed, traffic had to descend into the Tarn River valley and pass along the route nationale N9 near to the town of Millau, causing ridiculously heavy congestion at the beginning and end of the July and August peak school holiday season. Millau was then known and dreaded as a 'great black spot' of motoring. These slowdowns meant that the advantages of the A75 were completely lost. The A75 was meant to be a positive example of spatial planning, a modern, direct highway entirely free along its 340 km length. As it was, the traffic from the autoroute used to bring pollution and danger to the whole region. But now, since 2004, the bridge traverses the Tarn valley above its lowest point, linking the Causse du Larzac to the Causse Rouge, linking with the Grands Causses regional natural park.

We looked again at the map.

"Look," I said to H. "The bridge is actually the last link of the A75 autoroute (*la Méridienne*) coming from Clermont-Ferrand. So, I suggest we head towards the tiny airport at Rodez then on the N88 follow the signs to the A75 autoroute. This way we can drive south towards Millau so that we don't miss driving over the bridge itself. Being thrifty I had also heard that there shouldn't be any tolls to pay, other than just before the bridge.

To us, it sounded like a really nice drive. We were all looking forward to it.

We set off early in the morning, so as to make good time. I had prepared a picnic lunch for all of us consisting of the usual vegetarian options of quiches, hot crusty bread, cheese and home-grown tomatoes (our first), but with an added bag of Vienna-like sausages for the boys!

The route to Rodez was uneventful until we hit the tricky problem of a road sign with one arrow pointing to Rodez centre, the other to Millau. As usual I chewed over which direction to take. I knew we didn't want to go to Rodez centre, but neither did we want to head south to the village of Millau, thereby missing the thrill of actually driving on the road-bridge itself. Eventually we plumped for the Millau sign, and were soon rewarded, a few kilometres further on, with another sign pointing to the A75. Hugh sighs of relief.

We decided to stop for lunch at a particularly picturesque spot. Our daughter and I unloaded the picnic hamper from the boot of the car, careful not to also unload Bruno loose onto the country lanes, never to be seen again. We tied the panting Bruno to a nearby tree and sat on our chequered wool blanket.

All around we could see fields and fields of glorious sunflowers. From my time in the Botany Department at the university, I knew that the botanical name for the flower was *Helianthus*, the greek word *helios* meaning sun and *anthos* meaning flower. I supposed that the flower was really named after the sun which it resembles.

We turned our heads. Far into the distance, as far as the eye could see, were these giant yellow flower heads with their enormous dark centres and bright yellow petals. Each flower seemed to be pushing its head thirstily towards the glorious rays of the Mediterranean sun. I didn't blame them. I felt exactly the same. Every newspaper I ever read strictly enjoins us to avoid, at all costs, any glimmers of sunshine. Yet, how can it be wrong when one's sense of well-being is magnificently enhanced every time we're fortunate enough to show our faces to its warming rays?

H agrees with me, ever since he read in the Telegraph that exposure to sunshine actually reduces the risk of men getting prostate cancer. Enough said. And I even read the unlikely fact that sunflower stems were used to fill lifejackets before the advent of modern materials, so I'll be all right then if ever I venture on board a ship again! But clearly, the French grow their sunflowers for the seeds and oil they produce. Apparently each mature flower yields nearly half of its weight as oil.

Having finished our picnic, we cleared up the debris, fed the dog and packed everyone and Bruno back into the car, ready for the remainder of the journey. We soon reached the A75 and headed southwards towards Montpellier. Everything seemed to be going smoothly, before we hit our first big problem. As always. We came to a green exit sign pointing towards Millau and as we rapidly approached we all argued over whether we should take it or not. H shouted: "Hurry up. Do you want me to take this exit or not?" We dithered, before H eventually took matters into his own hands and took the Millau exit.

Wrong!

We ended up in the heart of the village of Millau, amidst congestion, traffic, children, workers and narrow alleyways too tiny to make detours. Eventually we found some signs with a small 'i' information sign and the picture of a viaduct, so we followed them. These certainly led us to the viaduct bridge, but from miles underneath, where we could only crane our necks upwards in disbelief.

"But, I wanted to actually drive over it," H said. We all decided to ask inside the information centre. We pushed open the doors and entered into a typical tourist information office. In my best French I asked:

"Le Viaduc?"

"Oui"

"Je voudrais conduire sur le pont. C'est quelle direction?"

The assistant looked puzzled, evidently confirming her long-standing belief that *les anglaises* were all congenitally stupid. "C'est là-bas," over there, pointing outside.

"Non. Vous n'avez pas compris," I countered, annoyed at her stupidity in not understanding my excellent French. "Je ne voudrais pas regardez le pont; je voudrais aller sur le point." How could she not understand that we didn't want to stare up at the bridge, we wanted to actually drive over it.

With a sigh of exasperation, the assistant handed to me a leaflet written in childish English and turned to the next tourist in the queue. We all wandered outside again, still mesmerised by the splendour of the seven enormous concrete pillars standing so proudly right in front of us. With hands tented over our eyes, we peered up into the sky. We could clearly see vehicles driving over the eight-span roadway so far above us, but how to get onto it?

When even the car-park attendant didn't understand either, giving the usual gallic shrug, we set off ourselves hoping to find the A75 sign and this time the northern route to Clermont-Ferrand – thereby still having a chance of driving over the bridge but from the opposite direction.

Success! We've done it. As with all things French, there was a lack of American razzmatazz or fanfares, no dancing girls with ra-ra skirts and pom-poms, not even a sign to tell drivers what they are about to see. Drivers approaching the many-barriered toll entrance to the famous site are not even regaled with advertising material, merely the amount of the toll that we needed to pay. We drove through and paid the attendant the necessary coins before suddenly, amazingly, we were actually on it. We drove as slowly as we could over the comparatively short length of the span so that we didn't miss anything. I had read that the special plastic barriers either side of the road-bridge had been erected to stop drivers becoming sea-sick(!) when they glanced down into the valley. Good job I wasn't driving then.

All too soon we had achieved our dream and were turning our heads homewards again. The sun was still shining, the sunflowers were still nodding their heads and the world had righted itself again.

We're all having a wonderful time, lazily swimming in our brand-new pool. Such luxury, such decadence, thinking about all those poor souls frantically working hard back home. As I laze on my back in our new swimming shorts and tankini top — great for hiding the vagaries of ancient bikini-lines and crepey legs – I suddenly puzzle over why H seems to have fixed a security label right underneath the water line where you can't read it. I shout out my question.

"It's because that was the only place it would stick to the liner without coming off."

"Oh," puzzled. I decided to dive underneath the water to read what it said.

"No diving!"

"For goodness sake."

After a glorious twenty minutes of swimming and lazily floating on my back, I was brought back to the present by the realisation that I could now see four rungs of the pool ladder instead of the usual three. I call out to him indoors:

"H, H, are you there?"

I hear a grunt from inside the barn, where a disembodied voice swears from somewhere behind the filtration unit.

As yet another rung of the step-ladder becomes visible above the rapidly receding waterline, we all beat a hasty retreat before disappearing down the virtual plug-hole. We rush into the barn to see what's going on, only to find H struggling with the heavy lever of the unit. I peer closely at it.

"No, no," exasperated. "You've got it pointing to *faire écouler*, the French word for 'drain.'"

"Well, how was I to know?" said he, suddenly chuckling to himself.

"What's so funny?" I was not amused, having spent so long in trying to make our new lifestyle so attractive to our family visitors.

"Well, I just remembered when, back in the market hall, my fishmonger neighbour was late in one morning and I posted a notice on his unit saying "Marooned. Back at high tide.""

Typical.

Before the family returns to the UK and the US again, we're all going to visit the town of Cordes sur Ciel. We couldn't wait. It's a lovely *bastide* village in our region, with four fortification lines.

We loaded the family in our two separate cars and hupped Bruno into the back, restrained by our new doggie guard. That's its supposed intention, but somehow Bruno has so far managed to chew his way through half of it. Oh well. The temperature outside was ninety degrees, so we opted for the air-con rather than opening all the windows. I read somewhere that opening the windows is no lighter on fuel consumption – each method has a similar drag on the fuel.

En route, the only sound was the panting of the dog in the back, followed by shouting from the driver: "Leave the car alone, you bloody dog!" Normal times then.

En route, because our American son-in-law was particularly keen on historical ruins (like his mother-in-law, then!), we stopped at *l'abbeye de Beaulieu* or *Belloc* in the Occitan language. He was fascinated to hear that during the Hundred Years War, especially towards its end, the abbey was almost totally destroyed. Hordes of routiers or armed warriors pillaged and ruined everything in their way. The church was looted and stripped of all its hangings, the gothic cloister was razed to the ground and the wings of the monks' quarters and refectory badly damaged. Now restored, the keystone centrepiece of the magnificent architecture represents the Paschal lamb. The number seven is of particular importance to the abbey. We saw seven rose windows, the one on the façade having seven points and the North arm of the transept rose window is composed of seven circles. Interestingly, though, there is a Star of David and Salomon's Seal situated in the South transept, which of course has six points, remaining the only exception to the number seven rule.

On leaving, I noted that on the opposite side, in the North transept, was an arrow pointing to the Portal of the Dead. A plaque described it as having been discovered only in 1963 and was completely brought to light during restorative works in 1979 of the North chapel. It gave me the shivers, so I begged off looking at that, glad to be out in the bright sunshine of twenty-first century France and our new life again.

Everyone packed back into our vehicles, we motored on through the rolling, green countryside of the Tarn et Garonne countryside, making a fine detour towards one of the *plus belles villages de France* called Les Cabannes. These *plus belle* signs are actively sought after by all villages in France, but only the best are awarded the coveted title and allowed to display the national sign.

On arrival at Cordes, everything looked magnificent, as always. The terrain all around the cité was very high, stony lanes impossibly steep leading up in a circuitous route past the ancient castle turrets, high up into the hills. The scenery all around was breathtaking, undulating hills and fields of green and gold, shimmering in the summer haze. High up in the trees, swallows and swifts swooped and dived on the air currents, searching and hunting for those myriads of delicious tiny insects that were their staple diet. In the full heat of summer, the insects buzzed and flitted, flying higher and higher in those cooler air drafts, pursued and hunted by the chasseur birds. That was the way of things: nature in all its terrible but wondrous glory.

The ancient town with its *Porte de l'horloge* and seriously steep cobbled streets, all combined to fill us with a heady thrill at the history that surrounded us. On the roadside there was a plaque which stated that Cordes, long before it would become part of France, received its charter in 1222 as a Bastide from the Count of Toulouse during the Occitan reconquest after the death of Simon de Montfort, the Lion of the Crusade. Someone said that the name was thought to be a derivative of the Indo-European root 'corte' meaning 'rocky heights.' And as names go, it certainly seemed appropriate because on a day like today, Cordes sat way above the clouds that blanketed the valley below.

Legend had it, that the original site chosen by the Count of Toulouse for the village to replace Saint-Marcel, was on

Puech (hilltop) Gabel. A local workman, sitting at the café, told us that when the original foundations for the town walls had been laid out, workmen had gathered materials, mixed mortar and carried stone to the site. After the first day's work they retired for the night. The next morning, they arrived at the building site only to find the previous day's work completely demolished. This apparently continued for thirty days, when a workman, in his frustration, threw his trowel in the air. Once he regained his composure he searched for it, but to no avail. It was found days later by a shepherd on a neighbouring hilltop. This was taken as a sign that the village should be built on that site. The workman told him that this was how Cordes came to be built on the heights of Mordagne. Over the following centuries, cloth, wool and leather crafts, as well as trade and finance, brought prosperity to the city. But in later years, plague devastations and the opening of the Canal du Midi caused the local population to drop to just two thousand by the time of the French Revolution.

Sunk in thought we walked over to *le petit train* station. I hadn't seen such a thing since childhood. We wondered whether they would take Bruno, and if so, whether they would charge for him. The train clanged round the corner, the driver cheerfully ushering all the waiting travellers on-board.

"C'est combien pour le chien?"

"Rien."

Phew.

I was so glad of the train as it somehow managed to work up enough steam to climb the amazingly narrow, one-in-ten gradient up to the citadel at the top. En route we passed our new dentist's surgery. H said that he always made his dental appointment for 2:30 – tooth-hurty! Sucking our teeth, we trundled on up the hill.

I now knew why it was called *Cordes sur Ciel*. We really felt as though we were on top of the world. After we had duly admired the magnificent view, we stopped for lunch at one of the many bistros dotted around *la place de la Halle*. After negotiating our way through the extensive à la carte menu, some of us plumped for the reasonably-priced *plat du jour* of *melon glace au porto*, followed by *côtes d'agneau grilees aux herbes*, or specially-arranged mushroom pasta with tomatoes for the vegetarians, then *dessert au choix*. Afterwards, the family asked me whether they should tip, always a complex problem. I knew that the practice wasn't as widespread as in the USA, where for many young waiters and waitresses, the tip can be their only source of income. However, here in France I usually looked for the words *service compris* on the bill, which usually meant that it was already included. What I tended to do, though, was to leave a few euros anyway — just to be sure. Always a worrier.

H was joking with his American son-in-law: "Did you know that in the UK you pay the bill with a cheque, but in the US you pay a check with a bill!"

After this my daughter and I wandered down some of the alleyways and spotted a fragrant soap and perfumerie shop. H tied Bruno securely to a shady lamppost outside as we went in. Some time later, as my daughter and I were standing in line waiting to pay for our purchases, we heard a strange clanging noise, which seemed to bang and thump all the way down the cobbled street. It didn't sound like *le petit train*, and any way I didn't think this was its normal route. We turned our heads just in time to see our son-in-law charging past the window at full tilt.

What on earth?

Hurriedly paying for our purchases, we dashed outside and looked down the hill. Sure enough there was our son-in-law and, wasn't that Bruno just ahead of him, charging down the hill with a huge iron lamppost in tow?

Now I had two comedians in the family: husband and Bruno.

However was I to survive?

21
Two on a boat (to say nothing of the dog)

"On a fine Sunday it presents this appearance nearly all day long, while, up the stream, and down the stream, lie, waiting their turn, outside the gates, long lines of still more boats; and boats are drawing near and passing away, so that the sunny river ……… is dotted and decked with yellow, and blue, and orange, and white, and red, and pink. All the inhabitants ………… dress themselves up in boating costume, and come and mouch (sic) round the lock with their dogs, and flirt, and smoke, and watch the boats; and, altogether, what with the caps and jackets of the men, the pretty coloured dresses of the women, the excited dogs, the moving boats………the pleasant landscape, and the sparkling water, it is one of the gayest sights I know…"

From "Three Men in a Boat (to say nothing of the dog)" by Jerome K. Jerome

The Occitan village lay sleeping, nestled in the snug maternal valley of the Aveyron. The cooling waters gurgled along their timeless flow, ebbing and trickling around the snake-like curves of the valley, then onto a smooth stretch, when suddenly with a sharp intake of breath they precipitously plunged down an unexpectedly steep weir to land with a roar and a splash into the pebbly bed beneath. The river told its own story: despite watching over the stupidities of man since time immemorial, it continued with its own superior path, ignoring the uncivilised behaviour all around, intent only on its own watery purpose and translucently clear vocation.

Chez-nous all was breathless anticipation. The two of us

had been invited to a French Regatta by the village social committee, the invitation stating clearly that we should attend dressed in straw hats and whatever boating paraphernalia we owned. The setting was to be the nearby stretch of the Aveyron river, a well-known haunt for boating enthusiasts of every hue, colour and creed, and we couldn't wait. At the foot of the invitation, it said that we should bring a picnic, table and chairs, the picnic to be partaken after the various boating competitions had been concluded. "Good," I thought; we can use that picnic set that was given to me when I left work. Rather like the tardis in Dr. Who, it has an amazing array of implements buried deep within its sturdy canvas lining. Whenever you think you've found all that it has to offer, out regurgitates yet more. To date I have discovered all kinds of plates, cutlery, cheese board, champagne glasses, champagne bottle holder and corkscrew, but lately I discovered a funny gadget which I think is a garlic press. I dare say more will be revealed in due course.

The whole day sounded like marvellous fun and even him indoors had difficulty in hiding his anticipation as we waited to see what kind of weather was in-store for us. This was despite his oft-cited comment that boats were really just a hole in the water into which you poured money! Why would anyone want to own a boat? he had often said to me in the past. I mean, all you can do is sail up the bloody river and down the bloody river......

Sunday dawned, marvellously blue and warm. Heavens be praised. I don't know what the organisers would have done if there'd been one of those regular frightening thunderstorms we have every so often round here. Last Friday was a case in point. All day a heavy pall of dark clouds had been pushing steadily downwards, the air heavy and still. Not a breath of wind stirred, nor a voice to be heard from the myriad of creatures in the woods behind us. You can always tell when a storm is brewing by the actions of the old lady in the lane behind our house. She nips out at a steady pace, shutting and barring all the heavy wooden *volets* to her house before nipping back in again. I could picture her now, lying in wait for the inevitable. I have learned to my cost that whenever the old lady shuts her shutters, that is the time to unplug my computer. The weather pays scant regard for crashing computer programmes!

On that particular Friday, the storm broke at around teatime, the first fat raindrops beginning to plash downwards onto our terrace and stone table. All was quiet, every sensible person safely ensconced indoors, Bruno lying in the *sous-sol*, whimpering softly. Suddenly a jagged lightening bolt struck with diagonal force, followed almost instantaneously by the loudest bang I have ever heard this side of world war two. I thought the windows would shatter, so strong was the vibration throughout our house. Rather like Tchaikovsky's Fifth, the heavens resounded to wave after wave of crashes and bangs, the bedroom where we cowered intermittently lit up by the searing blue of the flashes. The earlier mild drizzle had now become a downpour, and a short way across the fields the sturdy oak, elm and sinewy poplars were rendered vulnerable for an instant in a momentary white blaze, almost simultaneous with that crack of thunder.

Him indoors and me rushed outside, late as usual, in an attempt to shut our wildly-swinging *volets*, but it proved extremely difficult as what seemed like a hurricane-strength storm battered the house from all angles. But, as with everything round here if you're patient, the storm eventually receded, followed in its wake by hours and hours of relentless pounding rain. For a long while we had both been silent as we listened to the gusting wind and the throbbing patter of the rain. When all was quiet again, we opened the window gingerly. Washed and cleansed by the storm, the air poured in cool breaths through the open window, blowing in from the surrounding fields a scent of saturated soil, fresh and renewed. We listened; the wind had now thankfully diminished and the thunder slowly, quietly grumbling way in the distance. Very soon all that could be heard from the pitch-black outside was a gentle breeze and the occasional slick murmur of wet tyres as a distant vehicle risked the village street. The following day dawned bright and clear, as if the storm had never been. Such is life.

But today was fine. There was no sign of a storm brewing, only the relentless summer sunshine beaming down upon all and sundry. Even Bruno sensed the excitement, running round and round the garden, tail cocked at a jaunty angle, ready for whatever these senseless humans had ordained for him.

We packed the picnic, table and chairs and dog into the car, not forgetting him indoors, and set off for the river. H looked handsome in his jaunty straw boater, resplendent in his beloved striped jacket à la Dougie Millins of London and jazzy cravat, a veritable character out of Renoir's 'Moulin de la Galette.' Pictured against the summer-blue azure sky, the clashing colours of his ensemble was an impressionist's dream, ecru vying with ochre vying with vermilian and verdigris. In contrast I looked almost drab, dressed in white trousers and a sailor-blue striped top. We did wonder what kind of boats would be provided, but presumed that all that would have been organised by the organising committee.

We found the spot without our usual unplanned diversions and drew to a halt on the stony path leading up to the wooden jetty. We unloaded our gear, quickly setting up our table and chairs under a shady tree on the earmarked grassy park alongside the river. The chairman of the organising committee was standing underneath a striped umbrella, leafing through a sheaf of papers strewn on top of a green baize tripod table. Around his neck hung a heavy brass horn, the kind not seen since the days of phonographs and twirling moustaches. We walked up in some trepidation.

"Nom?"

We told him, and asked whether Bruno could come too.

"Oui. C'est à vous à decider." I'd heard that before. As H would undoubtedly say, it usually preceded a paying opportunity. But no. It seemed that today there was no charge for members of *le club*. We smiled as he placed a tick by our names and went to chat to the other villagers gradually arriving on the scene, proffering cheeks in readiness for the lusty kisses. Such trials we go through.

Soon, it appeared that each person was to be paired with a name drawn out of the organiser's hat. Oh no! That simply hadn't occurred to us. What were we going to do with Bruno? We waited whilst various names were called out, then my name was pronounced with a heavy gallic accent. I was to be paired with a hearty Belgian called Georges, a man who laughed at every utterance I made, funny or not. Good job he hadn't been paired with H or they'd never get off the starting blocks. I wasn't too pleased to see that H had been paired with a busty Dutch lady called Helga, but he seemed happy enough. Well, he would, wouldn't he?

We all walked over to the jetty and looked down at the array of boats. I say boats, but on close inspection it was clear they were really canoes, painted in every colour under the sun. Each canoe had three wooden planks within, one fore, one aft with one across the middle. H discussed the matter with Helga and they decided that they would take Bruno, who could sit on the central plank.

My heart skipped a beat.

With a loud toot on the horn, the moustachioed chairman called each competitor to the jetty and we all clambered aboard. Whilst willing volunteers held our allotted canoe, I gingerly stepped aboard only to find that the unexpected extra load moved the boat away from the jetty. I was left in the somewhat compromised position of having one foot on the jetty, the other in the canoe — legs spread apart as if about to do a bout of physical jerks or even be pulled like a chicken wishbone! The volunteers struggled to manoeuvre the boat back to the jetty again and, my legs thankfully having regained their rightful position, Georges leapt in. He indicated that it would be better for me to sit to the fore, which would be the holding position, whilst he sat in the rear to do the steering. With my physique (somewhat overblown in the chest region) I soon decided to change to a more appropriate kneeling position. This way I could attempt to get some leverage on the oar as I swept the water first one side then the other. However, H didn't look too happy at the visual image of the lofty rump I was giving to my companion

165

immediately behind.

All canoes jostled and manoeuvred to the starting line, just in front of a horizontal row of colourful balloons, which would also act as the finishing post on the way back. Before the off, I just had time to hear the heavy panting from Bruno, tongue hanging to one side, as he pawed anxiously at the wooden floor of H's canoe alongside ours. But there was no time for thoughts of changing our minds. Soon, with brass horn quivering at his lips, the chairman tooted and the race was on.

Concentrate, girl, concentrate. I'm trying, I'm trying.

But despite Georges' and my strenuous efforts, no matter how hard we tried, the canoe kept revolving in ever-convoluting circles. As soon as we, with much effort, managed to right it and plough on regardless, the boat would turn yet again. I think the problem was caused by the disparity in arm strength between me and my partner. He was oaring heavily on one side, whilst I was managing to pirouette in another.

Eventually we managed the difficult manoeuvre of paddling around the floating balloons at the half-way point, in a position just ahead that of H, Helga and a panting Bruno. Suddenly, as if we hadn't enough troubles of our own, I heard a loud splash to my right. I just had time to see Bruno doggie-paddling past me at a rate of knots, soggy tail aloft acting as rudder, with a sinking and blubbering H floundering helplessly behind. There seemed no sign of Helga at all. But Georges and I had no time for sightseeing. We had a race to win. Other boats seemed also to be in trouble, so we ploughed relentlessly on, now well past the half-way point and battling our way towards the colourful finishing line.

With a loud toot, it looked as though, amazingly, Georges and I had come in third. We struggled heroically out of the boat to much applause from the sensible bystanders who had decided not to compete, and I tented my hand over my eyes in an attempt to see what had happened to H and Bruno. By this time all the other boats had now come limping in, many looking very thankful indeed to have even found the finishing line. But still no sign of the missing team. The organisers were just about to call out the *pompiers*, when a sorry sight suddenly hove into view. There was the boat, coasting slowly homewards again half-full of river water, its crew of H, Helga and Bruno a soggy antidote to the day's frolics.

But at least Georges and I must have won something, hadn't we? Well, no. Unfortunately, our hopes of a dashing cup to display proudly on our mantlepiece were dashed when the organiser told us in no uncertain terms that 'vous et votre mari, les deux étiez rendu incapable de gagner.'

"Why are both H and I disqualified?" I asked in disbelief.

"You and Monsieur are both disqualified, madame, because you and your companion did not successfully negotiate the balloons at the half-way point, and your husband — it is against the rules to fall in the water, bail out the boat and lose one's companion into the bargain."

Somehow, after that, despite winning the wooden spoon, it wasn't just the *cornichons* in our picnic that left a somewhat sour taste in our mouths.

But at least we lived to sail another day.

22
The market place

Every Sunday morning we make a point of going to the large market in the neighbouring town. It is always a revelation.

The market was in full swing when we arrived one particular Sunday, breathless from the pursuit of the recalcitrant Bruno. We knew from long experience, though, that because of the narrow streets and tourists in the summer period, it was better to leave the dog in the car. As we walked up the hill and glanced behind us, his hound-dog expression told its very own tale, or tail.

Walking over the picturesque old bridge, elegantly spanning the broad expanse of the river, it looked to me as if time had stood still. Despite the uncertainties of our new life here, the water sparkled and darted under the stone archways as evidence of time's infinite longevity, a spectacle so precious that even I, someone who was a congenital worrier, couldn't help but enjoy. All the abundance that nature can bring was all around us. We leaned a while on the old rough-hewn bridge and admired the many flowering baskets of bright pink geraniums, vying with cascading purple petunias and firebright begonias, that adorned the many arches.

"Why haven't they been stolen?" asked the realistic one next to me.

I agreed with him. This was another world, another time. Greeting strangers with a nod of the head and a *bonjour*, made me think of England fifty years ago. It was one of the many things that I missed from my childhood days of the '50s.

Quickly reaching the crowded market place, we ambled and elbowed our way through the multifarious summertime throng. Everywhere, English people abounded.

"Darling, just take a look at this,"

and

"Darling, how quaint......"

H grumbled to me: "I wish all these English foreigners would go home again!"

I smiled to myself as we eyed the colourful wares on display. Today I was looking for a new wicker basket. This commodity is almost a badge of honour on the elbow of every local French woman. It reeked of gallic charm and old-fashioned values and ideals. It was one of the first items I had purchased on arrival in France, so that I would be ready to integrate into the French style of living. But Bruno had unfortunately got to it first and chewed his way through the base. I could no longer trust the basket to hold all the produce without emptying its contents all over the road.

So, with a sigh I walked down to the first basket stall. Let's hope the owner isn't himself a basket-case. I began my opening gambit to the bemused trader:

"Regardez celui-ci," pointing to the frayed and chewed base of my basket. "C'est le chien qui a le mangé."

The trader studied the basket and agreed with me. "Tok. Ça, ce n'est pas bien."

"Um, je cherche quelque-chose avec un base plus fort....vous comprenez?"

"Oui madame." He hunted through his multifarious merchandise, selecting then discarding before finally plumping for a rounder, more solid version.

"Voilà!" handing me a pretty basket, threaded through with flaxen threads of red, ochre and green, but with a much stronger base and handle.

"How much?" asked H.

"Vent," said the trader in heavily-accented French.

H rooted in the purse and handed over eighteen euros.

The trader looked first offended, but then — after pausing awhile — agreed and put our money into his deep apron pocket. Transaction duly recorded, he wished us *un bon Dimanche*, before turning to his next customer.

All's fair in love and war.

We walked onto the next stall, a fruit and vegetable bazaar, where I proceeded to fill my new basket with all the many-hued produce on display. There were bright purple aubergines and sun-kissed tomatoes *en grappe*. You could smell their pungent fragrance from afar. There were giant peaches, their skins furry and succulent, alongside home-grown strawberries, hairy pink raspberries and juicy fruit of every size, texture and hue. We paid for our produce and were just about to turn away when suddenly I heard a slight commotion. Ducking my head under a bench, I saw what the disturbance was: a clucking brown hen surrounded by white eggs, still warm.

This is what I loved. The rich varieties, sizes and shapes of all the fruit and vegetables, the home-grown produce, the warm fresh eggs straight from the farm. I must admit I hate anything uniform, regimented.....reminds me too much of my old working life at the university.

We crossed the street, narrowly avoiding collision with a group of pink-faced tourists with various baby-buggies in tow. We ducked down a dark alley and found the cool, dusty *cave* we had discovered on our last trip. Having come prepared, H fished out from under his arm a large white plastic jerrican with a spout and walked over to the man serving *vin en vrac* direct from the oaken riveted casks.

"Le plein, s'il vous plait," he parroted proudly. Fill it up, please. It was one of the first phrases he learned over here. As he always said, it is a very useful phrase. You can use it for wine, at the garage, at the bank……..

Rather like an old-style garage attendant of yore, the wine merchant opened the taps and filled our canister with affordable fresh local red wine direct from a hosepipe, glugging the bottle right to the top before twisting the cap tight and handing it back to us. The French have always liked real, true produce and this kind of thing has always appealed to them. You know what you're getting and can clearly see what your money is buying.

"You should ensure you drink this within a few months, or

immediately if you extract some from the container," he told us.

I looked at H and agreed with the trader that we would be sure to keep to his wise instructions.

"No problem," said H.

Wine traders like this one usually buy their wine in bulk direct from producers such as wine co-operatives *(caves cooperative)* and wine-growing unions. The wholesale price can be as little as eighty centimes per litre for a good *vin de pays*, costing around one euro, sixty in a labelled bottle in a supermarket.

One of the pleasures of living in France for wine lovers is being able to visit a vineyard on a sunny day and celebrate *la culture du vignoble*. We were told that appointments must be made to visit some *châteaux* and most are closed during lunchtimes (*naturellement*). On these visits the quality of wine people are invited to taste often seems to depend on one's ability to make the right comments, and whether you appear to be rich! Wine tasting has its own unique vocabulary, difficult in any language, so if not a wine connoisseur, it's probably best to stick to bon, très bon and even, if really impressed, très très bon.

Before we left the market, H insisted on stocking up on some spirits, which are cheaper in France than in many other European countries, although dearer than in Italy and Spain. Looking around, I could see his mouth watering at the selection. There was cognac, Armagnac (a speciality of this region), marc (a grape brandy from Burgundy), calvados (an apple brandy from Normandy), kirsch (a cherry brandy from Alsace) as well as a wide variety of liqueurs such as Bénédictine, Chartreuse, Cointreau and Grand Marnier. There were also the aniseed liqueurs of absinthe and *pastis* such as Pernod and Ricard which are brewed in the south.

Looking around, H whispered: "I wonder why they call this one here *Pissenlit*?"

"Shh," I countered, embarrassed.

With so much choice all around, he decided against the Scotch whisky. Why buy imported, when there were so many home-grown varieties.

We walked out onto the hot streets again, ducking under the brightly-striped, gaudy awnings of the shop-fronts. As we walked back to the car, I mused that French open weekly markets like this one are so much better than the vagaries of a regular supermarket. I knew that I could get by in this country with my basic French, but there were so many linguistic pitfalls in the supermarket. *Conservateur* or *agent de conservation*, for example, is a preservative. However, *sans préservatifs* means "without condoms!"

Don't tell H, whatever you do.

The word *organique* is a branch of chemistry and does not refer to organic food — that is called *bio* pronounced bee-o (not B.O.!), short for biologique. Colour-coding on milk bottles is different from the UK, as I discovered to my cost. The blue tops are demi-créme and red tops full cream. How ever am I to lose weight with such confusion. I also discovered that *un paquet de persil* is not a packet of detergent, but a bunch of parsley, and if you don't want to turn your butcher into hysterics, don't call chicken legs 'jambes', but 'cuisses.'

Next, we wended our way through the throngs to the Boulangerie. Since the nineteenth century French law has decreed that all towns and villages above a certain size must have a Boulangerie or an outlet selling bread. Indeed, many an old country home has its own bread oven still. The price and weight of bread is still regulated by government, keeping it uniform throughout France. Un *pain* or *parisien* must weigh four hundred grams and a *baguette* two hundred grams. All bread in France must be freshly made, because it goes stale very quickly. That is why bakers bake twice or sometimes three times every day. Artisans offer their own specialised varieties to their own recipes. We particularly like the black bread, thickly encrusted with rye and cereal grains. As if I didn't know, the Boulangerie also makes and sells *croissants*, *brioches* (like a sweet bun), assorted breads made with walnuts, hazelnuts, almonds or raisins, together with the most delicious cream *pâtisserie*. The most important thing to remember is that all Boulangeries close one day a week. If we forget, we don't have any dough!

In May 07 France celebrated its twelfth *Fête du Pain* with bread-themed events taking place across the country. In France, to become a baker is an art in itself. It is necessary to become an apprentice from an early age. There is no other way to learn all the secrets of the trade. The first bread shift starts at 11 p.m. Many bakeries make as many as thirty-five different types of bread using a variety of pre-mixed flours. The flour for French bread is very different from British flour, which has a hard texture. The apprentice must take a fistful of flour and squeeze it into the hand. If it keeps its shape when you open your fist, you know the flour is the soft variety — considered by British bakers to be only good for *pâtisserie*. However, in France this variety is known as 'type 55' and is used for almost everything. For people with a gluten problem, this bread might be O.K. as its gluten content is very low. It loses all its elasticity if handled roughly, which would mean that the bread would not rise.

France is famous all over the world for the distinctive shape and freshly-made smell of its bread. Other than the *parisien* and *baguette*, other common varieties are the skinny one-hundred gram *ficelle* (piece of string), the *boule* (round loaf) and the *bâtard*, which is the same width as the *parisien* but much shorter.

The different types of bread can also be distinguished by their individual markings. *Un pain* normally has five slashes across the top, the same type with diamond-shaped slashes being called a *polka*. Some bakers use a black metal mould in order to bake six loaves at one time, each piece of dough laid side by side. For customers who like really crusty bread, i.e. those without false teeth!, then the *non-moulé* is the one to ask for. For people who like the kind of old-fashioned bread which has been made from unbleached flour, they should look for a sign saying "*Pain de tradition*." This type of bread is baked on the floor of the oven rather than in a special mould. These days most bakers use modern ovens, but there are still some rural bakers who still bake in wood-fired ovens: *au feu de bois*. In Paris there is a well-known one called *Poilane*.

Specialist breads using different types of bread are common. There are endless varieties. There are the *pain de campagne*, which is a country loaf made from a mix of rye and plain flour, a *pain complet*, made with wholemeal flour, a *pain de seigle*, rye flour, or a *pain brie*, which is baked with white flour but is heavily beaten, making it very dense. This type, so it is said, used to be taken to sea by fishermen, which they would eat with shrimps and salted butter. It is not unusual for the French to prepare their rye bread with oysters and salted butter, then toasted to serve hot with pat*é*. The best bakers, like *Poitrane* in Paris, regularly make large round country loaves which they decorate with leaves, bunches of grapes and tendrils.

For the children, *pain d'épice* is a favourite. It is gingerbread that should be honeyed and eaten for breakfast. Some bakers also use their *pain brie* to fashion different sorts of patterns to amuse and entice the children: sometimes little apples, grapes or lobsters, crabs and birds.

Years ago it was common for French housewives to buy their bread as many as three times a day, not just because they loved their bread piping hot, but because the bread went stale so quickly. Often *petits pains au lait* are bought for breakfast or dinner, and in the Basque country, pumpkin and corn bread are eaten with a cup of tea in the afternoon.

In Provence a speciality is the *pain de Beaucaire*. The baker cuts the dough into two rectangles, one on top of the other, then cuts it into squares, leaves it to rise and then bakes it on the side. Some bakers even use varieties made with cottage cheese or pears.

Of course, as with all things, the quality of the bread is entirely dependent on the artistry of the artisan. Each region of France has its specialities, starting with a fairly standard recipe, but then varied by the quality of the flour, the number of risings and the extra added ingredients and patterns.

For older people who remember a time during the depression or war years, many were the recipes which made

use of stale bread. Below is one of them:
La Panade de Gisele Caumon
Place the stale bread broken into pieces in a saucepan
Cover with chicken stock
Cook until soft and break up with a fork
Add salt, freshly ground black pepper
At the last minute, stir in two or three eggs and lightly cook
Add a spoonful of chopped parsley
Enjoy!

Apparently the word *pain* has nothing to do with the English word 'pain'! It originates from the Latin word *panis* meaning bread. First it evolved into *pan* in Old French and then slowly developed into its modern form by the thirteenth century. The word 'companion' or *compagnon* in French comes from the word *cum* combined with *panis*, meaning someone with whom you eat bread.

Every Easter the annual *Fête du n'oeuf* takes place in the village. Every year people come from far and wide to view the magnificent half-metre high eggs decorated by artists, artisans, school children and local organisations. The *Fête du n'oeuf* is co-ordinated by the Association Beffroi that is made up of local businesses, independent professionals as well as local artists and artisans. The aim of the association is to promote economic activity in the town and it organises amongst other things the Candle Festival at Christmas and the summer night markets — another amazing highlight of the year. The Easter Egg festival is now a fixed part of its annual programme of events, and when we visited it earlier in the year we were amazed as we walked around all the exhibits.

This year there were double the number of egg entries with about eighty on display on the streets in the heart of this mediaeval town. Displays were erected all along the cobbled rue de la Pelisserie through to the Place de la Halle. This year the festival was opened by the Maire followed by a free Apero under the covered market hall. H, please note. Taking a lead from the many tourists in the vicinity, it was clearly a great photo opportunity. We remembered seeing a board leaning against the wall of the Mairie advertising that that very afternoon would be a variety of activities such as an egg hunt where only children can enter and the 'giant omelette' that involves breaking several hundred eggs (only real eggs can enter). Later that evening there was a public auction of many of the eggs that had been on display. Someone told me that last year there were many eggs sold for from twenty euros right up to three hundred euros. All visitors are given a chance to vote for their favourite egg with different categories for artists and local organisations. It is clear that this egg festival has now become a must-see for people from all over the region and is set to grow in importance year on year.

The open market, with all its different foods, colour, vibrancy and atmosphere is a world apart from the often-bland and universal supermarkets. But above all, it allows you to see, taste and select your chosen produce at a price that's right, with specialised advice and knowledge from each individual trader. Additionally there are so many colourful activities for visitors to enjoy.

It may sound like an advert, but for me it's a whole new shopping experience!

23
Pétanque

After we had returned home from the wonderful open-air market, where nothing needs to be asked for — merely picked up, selected and haggled over by H, we had lunch then prepared to set out for our weekly game of pétanque. What we particularly like about this game is that you don't need to be fit to play. Why else would we play it!

Pétanque celebrated its one-hundredth birthday in June 07, but the origins of this most French of games go back much further. Archaeologists have found what they believe to be a set of boules in a child's sarcophagus in Egypt dated 5000 BC, and there are records of a similar game played in Greece at the time of Alexander the Great.

A version of boules was introduced to France by the Romans after the conquest of Gaul, and it has never looked back since. It took such a hold that by the Middle Ages Charles V of France – and even Edward III of England – banned soldiers from playing boules because it was interfering with their military training.

I had always wondered what the difference was between boules and the more modern pétanque. An old man in the village informed me that back in 1907 an elderly former champion called Jules le Noir went out to play. Because he suffered from arthritis, he drew a small circle in the sand and played with both feet firmly on the ground — *à pieds tanqués* as it was spoken in the local dialect. Onlookers so sympathised with Jules and his kyphotic spine that they too changed their normal one foot in front of the other stance, to the *pieds tanqu*és as Jules did. And so pétanque was born.

On July 17th 2007 at the boulodrome Jules le Noir at La

Cloitat, Marseille, the very place where the game was born, a special celebration was held, reconstructing that very first game of pétanque with Jules's two-footed throw. The game is now such a global phenomenon that it will be played at the 2012 Olympics.

Not being Olympians ourselves, we approached our first play with considerable trepidation. We had been invited by some English friends to play. It can be played anywhere from the back garden to the beach. However, most towns have official clubs and gravel sites in which all are welcome. It's certainly an excellent way for newcomers to France to meet new people and to learn to play this great game. It might even help H to improve his strategy and concentration, but you never know.

The game is competitive but not aggressive and players spend much of the time during a game chatting and socialising with each other — especially me on the day we turned up. It's perfect for those like us trying to improve their French – you have to communicate with your team mates and other players. On the day we arrived, we found ourselves playing with people who were native to the area, the inevitable English and some Dutch people who, like us, love it in the south of France.

Each player uses three boules when playing a *doublette* with one partner, or two boules when playing a *triplette* with two partners. A player from the winning team draws a circle about half a metre wide in the playing area and throws the small coloured jack, *cochonnet,* six to ten metres.

H puzzled everyone by throwing a pickled cucumber. Foolishly I asked him what he was playing at.

"Pétanque, of course."

"Yes, yes," exasperated, "but why did you throw that gherkin."

"Ah," he replied with an amused grin. "That's what they said we should throw, didn't they: *un cornichon*!"

"No, it's not a *cornichon* (gherkin) you idiot, but un *cochonnet!!"*

Anyway, we learned that both feet must be on the ground

within the circle. The player then throws his boule from either a crouching or upright stance, trying to get as close to the *cochonnet* (not the *cornichon!)* as possible. The opposing team must then try to get their boules as close as possible to the *cochonnet* and continue playing until they do. When they get closer it is back to the other team, and so forth. A player can choose to either 'place' his boule to get it near the *cochonnet* – in which case he is called a *pointeur*, or 'shoot' high in the air with force to try to knock the opponent's boule away, a *tireur*. Each team has a captain — usually the one with a good eye for crafty tactics. The winning team scores a point for each boule that is nearer the *cochonnet* than the opposing team's nearest boule. The art of the game is observing the lie of the land, each throw on the often heavily-shingled court falling differently.

H whispered: "It would be much better to use a *cornichon* as the jack because then, at the end of the game, the winner gets something to eat!"

Ignoring this ongoing banter, I must admit we had great fun with the game, especially when trying to argue a point with one of the experienced local French players! Well, we would wouldn't we?

As we left, I could still hear one of the locals called Jacques calling out, after I had placed a particularly good shot: "Ah, elle est belle." Of course, being naturally vain, for a moment I thought he was talking about me. Momentarily, I preened myself. But of course, as I soon realised he was describing my shot!

Oh well, I can dream can't I?

24
Brocantes Fair

We've just returned from our annual visit to the brocantes fair in our own village. It takes place along the Aveyron riverside, creating a wonderfully colourful scene for locals and tourists alike. Summer is definitely brocantes season round here. Every weekend from May to September you will find a car boot sale in progress in villages throughout the land, a festive occasion to which most of the village takes part.

The Maire's office is the organising point and some weeks beforehand posters are made and displayed in the surrounding area telling where people can book stalls and tables. Local villagers obtain their tables for practically nothing and even professionals don't have to dig too deep for the required euros. The events are often sponsored by business people who may live in the village, or a nearby garage, shop or church charity fundraising committee.

The week before, the organising team gets to work in earnest or in Paradis. Leaflets are distributed to each resident's postbox to say when and where those living in the locale will not be able to park their cars, and table areas are marked out on the riverside grassy verges with the numbers allocated to stallholders.

The local boulangerie always does a roaring or baking trade on brocantes days. They open their doors very early and often carry on non-stop until 6 p.m. The local shop and café also take a lot of money. Everywhere there is a carnival atmosphere and everyone is made most welcome.

On the day of the brocantes, activity starts early with the tables and stalls being erected and the salle des fêtes is sometimes opened for coffee and croissants for the organising team — all the able-bodied men and their wives who are on refreshment duty.

By 5 a.m. the first stallholders arrive and by 7 a.m. the event is in full swing with the early bird dealers ready to pounce pell-mell on any bargains. The early morning start also sees many Dutch, followed by the British. It's truly amazing what some people collect. One man told us that he and his son collected world war one memorabilia and his wife collected wooden butter pats. He proudly showed us his purchase of the day, to which he was justly proud: an unworn gas mask complete with its non-rusty tin and instructions for use. This treasure cost them all of one euro. H reckoned that it would probably have fetched thirty pounds back in his old market hall in England. Someone else told us that the previous year they had bought a 1960s electric guitar for the equivalent of twenty pounds, something that later was sold for one hundred and twenty pounds to a specialist guitar deal in the UK.

By twelve o'clock we were feeling hungry, so after buying an attractive wicker herb rack — something that would go rather well in our new kitchen — for two euros from a stallholder raising money for the local church restoration fund, we wended our way homewards again. On the main road, we turned right down an alleyway towards the castle ramparts and gate. We loved this part of the walk from the river and never failed to be impressed by the history all around us. Bruno was pulling hard and I was glad to take a rest on the stone seat under the arrow slits at the entrance to the old walled cité. These ancient arrow apertures were historical evidence of another time, another place, another mindset when the Cathars fought the French to protect the cité.

I tilted my neck back and gazed up at the top of the stonework. Tiny fan-tailed swifts were settled all in a row on the ancient masonry, before suddenly, as if on a whim, flying off in formation towards the river. For a moment, they reminded me of the military flying low overhead, but I shook my head free from my reverie. This was hardly a time of

world war.
　Merely the best time of our lives.

25
Size matters

How am I going to understand measurements in France?

Looking around me, everywhere are petite, tiny, slim women, short beds, strange kitchen utensils, metric sizes and land sizes in hectares.

Time to do some research so that me and him indoors can have something to go on (no, we've already covered the *fosse toutes eaux*, H.!). Let's see. It appears that the French system is metric rather than the old imperial system with which we are more familiar. And I dare say that French clothes manufacturers are every bit as diverse in their sizing as their English counterparts. At least most French shops appear willing to exchange items or even give refunds if they're feeling generous.

As with all women, I'm forever seeking those elusive women's clothes that make my figure look slimmer whilst at the same time flatter my better parts. But, *touts horreurs*, French sizes look horrendous. Whereas American women's sizes at least flatter my ego by having a number that appears to be two sizes smaller than in the UK (for instance, the UK size 16 is equivalent to the American size 14), the equivalent French size is an appalling size 42! And if, in truth, I balloon to a UK size 20 around the bust (always having enjoyed(!) a Diana Dors physique), although in America I would only be a size 18, in France I would be a size 46! Why didn't we emigrate to the US instead?

I'm in need of some relief from all this panic, so looked furtively in the windows of some shoe shops in the nearest big town. Trouble is, I have always had large feet and no matter how much I diet, they fail to get any smaller. Perhaps I should have been born in China centuries ago, where my grandmother would have done something about it, but as it is, they're here to stay. Let's see. I walked inside and picked up a shoe that more or less matched my own shoe size of eight and looked at the French size underneath: forty-two! That sounds enormous. I assumed that, following the pattern with women's clothes, that the American sizing would be smaller than the UK, but no. Even there, the nearest US size to the UK eight is ten.

And for men's feet, why does France assume that men's feet don't come any bigger than a standard size nine (UK)? Must be because French men only come in one standard size: small! But, if you shop around, I've found that it is possible to purchase size forty-six for him indoors with size eleven (UK) feet.

Note: If, like me you are a woman who takes UK size eight shoes, be prepared to have all your French socks in dull black, brown, white or grey (i.e. men's socks). Feminine pinks don't come in large sizes.

With woollens, I've discovered further anomalies to make my head reel. Taking my bust size as, say, forty in the UK, this is the same size in the US, but seems to compare with forty-six (!) in France. But the really strange thing is, and this makes no sense to me at all, why are men's chests presumed bigger than women's? I'd have thought there were obvious reasons to the contrary. Secondly, how can a woman's French size forty-six equal the UK size forty, but the men's size forty-six equal the UK size thirty-six? I would have expected the size forty-six to be the same in both cases, but what do I know?

And what about men's shirt sizes? The French either go for chest measurements rather than neck-sizes, or Frenchmen's necks are very big indeed.

Cooking measurements

Because the differences here are too difficult to describe, I've listed the important units below.

Imperial	Metric	Metric	Imperial
1 UK pint	0.57 litres	1 litre	1.75 UK pints
1 US pint	0.47 litres	1 litre	2.13 US pints
1 UK gallon	4.54 litres	1 litre	0.22 UK gallons
1 US gallon	3.78 litres	1 litre	0.26 US gallons
1 US 'cup'	0.25 litres or 250 ml.		

My late father always used to joke that the only thing in which the US was behind the UK was in clock-time. It now looks as though the US gallon and US pint are also slightly behind!

Note: Don't expect to find a measuring jug in heat-proof glass. They don't appear to exist in France. All cooking jugs seem to come in plastic, so don't attempt to put hot gravy or hot custard in them…come to think of it, why would you want to make gravy or custard in France??

Similarly, with oven temperatures, I've listed these below to avoid confusion. As we're in the land of *bien manger*, you'd better pay some attention to these if you're to perfect the cooking skills required.

Oven temperatures

Gas	Electric °F	°C	
-	225-250	110-120	(Log-burning temperatures not available)
1	275	140	
2	300	150	
3	325	160	
4	350	180	
5	375	190	
6	400	200	
7	425	220	
8	450	230	
9	475	240	
Too-high	burnt	burnt	

(Scouring pads at the ready)

Now we're getting into the swing of things, here are some weighty and lengthy measurements for you to digest.

Weight

Avoirdupois	Metric	Metric	Avoirdupois
1 oz	28.35g	1g	0.035 oz
1 lb	454g	100g	3.5 oz
1 cwt	50.8 kg	250g	9 oz
1 ton	1016 kg	500g	18 oz
2205 lb	1 tonne	1 kg	2.2 lb

Area

UK/US	Metric	Metric	UK/US
1 sq. in	0.45 sq. cm	1 sq. cm	0.15 sq. in
1 sq. ft	0.09 sq. m	1 sq. m	10.76 sq. ft
1 sq. yd	0.84 sq. m	1 sq. m	1.2 sq. yds
1 acre	0.4 hectares	1 hectare	2.47 acres
1 sq. mile	2.56 sq. km	1 sq. km	0.39 sq. mile

Length

UK/US	Metric	Metric	UK/US
1 in	2.54 cm	1 cm	0.39 in
1 ft	0.48 cm	1 m	3 ft 3.25 in
1 yd	91.44 cm	1 km	0.62 mile
1 mile	1.6 km	8 km	5 miles

France gets much hotter than in the UK, so you'd better understand the following too.

Temperature

°Celsius	°Fahrenheit	
0	32	Water freezing point
5	41	
10	50	
15	59	
20	68	
25	77	
30	86	
35	95	
40	104	
50	122	

If you're alive and reading this, then your body temperature should be 37°C or 98.4°F.

Boiling point of water is 100°C or 212°F.

If, for some reason, you want to convert Fahrenheit to Celsius, the quickest way is to subtract thirty from the Fahrenheit temperature and divide by two.

Conversely, if you want to convert Celsius to Fahrenheit, simply double the Celsius temperature and add thirty. Simple. A child could do it – even me!

***

So, there you have it.

You now have no excuse but to dress in the finest *haut couture*, wear sweaters in either over-large men's sizes or far-too-tight women's, pinch your feet in à la mode French shoes and burn your *haute cuisine* at the highest possible temperatures.

26
Sex à la français

May I then talk with thee as I was wont?
May I then hide my eyes in thy soft arms
After thy looks have made them tired of joy?
May I then play beside thee the long noons
When work is none in the bright silent air?
Percy Bysshe Shelley

We can't conclude this epistle about *la vie française* without talking about sex! We started thinking about it when we realised that we may have done a gross disservice to our dog Bruno. Everyone at the SPA in Montauban had insisted that we have him 'fixed' because of the ever-increasing numbers of unwanted dogs in France. We agreed because Madame had told us that, in her opinion, Bruno was a cross between a spaniel and a red setter, in view of his long legs. However, after talking to a few people in the know since, it could well be that Bruno is, in fact, a pure-bred gun dog who must have gone off the rails a bit. As H put it to me: "Just think what a fortune we might have made... It looks as if we might have recouped up to a thousand euros each time he was mated..." *Quel catastrophe!* Nothing we can do about it now, though, of course.

"Makes you think, though," mused H. "I mean, just think of the money I could make myself..."

"You mean, with you as gigolo?" aghast.
"Yeah, well, if there's that much money in it..."
"Yes, but knowing our luck, the thousand you might make each time would be in rupees!"

"How much is a thousand rupees, then?" interested.

"Oh, just about twelve pounds sterling!"

Whilst on the subject of sex, we thought again about the French. After all, when not eating, they are all supposed to be making love. They are internationally known to be obsessed with sex and have a long history of debauchery. Think of the Marquis de Sade, bordellos, French letters, the town of Condom, adultery and masturbation. Ironically, homosexuality is called here *le vice anglais,* even though their capital city, rife with transvestites, is known worldwide as 'gay Paris'.

In all innocence, as is our wont at our time of life and having led a very sheltered life, one Saturday evening we walked into a local bar to enjoy a quiet drink and take in the ambience of local culture. We gave no thought to a rather beautiful old cello standing idle in the corner. *Perhaps there'll be some music later*, I thought idly to myself as I looked around at the crowd of locals clustering around the bar.

Leaning up against the bar was a wooden hand-painted sign advertising Saturday evening musical sessions. Ah, that then was the reason for this sudden influx of people. We smiled indulgently to ourselves, until the attractive busty woman serving the drinks suddenly wiped her hands, lifted up the bar counter and tottered over to the cello in the highest heels I had ever seen. She was wearing a coral pink, figure-hugging dress, decadently split right up to the thigh, the bodice encrusted with glittering pearls. Her eyes were expertly but heavily made up à la Dusty Springfield, thick clusters of black mascara clinging to her upper and lower lashes, with gold dangly hoop earrings completing the ensemble.

As she ran to the cello and with a whoosh jumped astride the wooden chair placed before it, we wondered if we shouldn't have moved a little further away, but it was too late now. Any change of seats now would be an insult to the musician.

As the lilting strains of a Jacqueline du Pré wafted around

the room , filling our ears with a haunting ambience, H strangely seemed busy studying the musician. Well, he couldn't do much else sat where he was. I could see him staring fixedly at two almost bare thighs as she sat astraddle the wooden chair, the skirts of her dress straining hugely across her lower regions. Having come to a momentous decision, H leaned over to me and whispered in my ear:

"I think she's a man — or rather he," he mouthed.

"What? No!"

"Oh yes," he said, finger tapping the side of his nose. "I think by now I can tell the difference…"

And he was right. Now I came to think of it, no woman would have leaped astride a seat in quite such an inelegant way. We women have learned from years of experience what to do with our legs when we sit. This woman, man or whatever he was, certainly hadn't yet learned that valuable art, his legs all akimbo either side of the rounded, almost womanly, curves of the cello. Now that I knew, I almost expected the musician to shout out "Whatcha mate" in recollection of Danny la Rue.

Later, having got used to the idea, but having enjoyed immensely the lilting strains of the music for the last hour, we walked over to the bar and chatted to her — sorry, him. It appeared that he was English. His name was Marie, née Mark, and he had led a very interesting life. Marie, formerly known as Mark, came to France being fed up with work as a builder in England. His brother was building in France and needed help so Mark said he would come for a couple of weeks; eleven years later he is still here.

In recent years work as a builder became impossible as fairly serious hormonal changes made Mark feel that he was a woman. In fact the hormone imbalance had a physical as well as a mental impact on his life. Impossible to work on a building site in a dress but Mark, now Marie, knew he still had to earn a living.

A lucky chance brought him to this bar at the same time as the owners were thinking of selling. (*Of all the bars in all the world, you had to come to this one…*). Mark jumped at the chance to step in and has worked hard for the last six months to make the bar and restaurant a success. Marie admits that she made a few mistakes at first but now with a new chef planning an exciting and international menu, she feels very positive.

Marie still has many problems to face including the prospect of a full sex change operation which her doctors are advising. We had to admit that listening to her story certainly changed our previous view on transvestites. Having listened carefully to her whole courageous story, we told her that whatever she decides to do in the future, we sincerely wished her well.

That night, lying in bed unable to sleep, I mulled long and hard on that emotive word 'sex'. I thought that if we're ever to get to grips with what it's like to be a Frenchman or woman, it's time we got to grips with French social customs, and not before time.

Let's start with kissing, so to speak. Much to H's annoyance, it is not the norm to kiss everyone on sight, especially not all the pretty girls. So, as he says, "to kiss or not to kiss, that is the question." As with all things, especially when playing snooker, you must take your cue from the French themselves.

When first introduced to an adult, do not *faire la bise* (kiss) on sight. Listen carefully, H. If a woman expects you to kiss her, she will offer you first her cheek, then if you are lucky.......But remember, men kiss women and women kiss women but men do not kiss men, unless they are very very close friends or called Mark. The kiss is placed high up on the offered cheek, never directly on the mouth. For women, especially, it's not really a kiss, merely a light brushing of the cheeks. Of course there are always the extroverts of both sexes who plant great wet smackeroos on each side of the face several times. But this is not to be recommended, especially not on first acquaintance.

"But, which cheek should I proffer first?"

Difficult to say. As with all things, observe what the locals do, as the custom apparently varies from region to region.

"How many kisses are *de rigeur*?"

In our region we discovered that three is the custom, much to H's delight. I had heard that Thomas Cook had actually published a kissing guide, though I had never discovered it in any of the local newsagents. It allegedly states that a single kiss is the norm in the Charente-Maritime region, two kisses are normal in the east, west and extreme south, three kisses in the mid-west and southern central regions and four in the north. "When can we move to the north?" Grr.

Mulling again about that emotive word sex, I thought about the French women I had met so far in this strange alien world. French women don't seem to have heard of Germaine Greer or feminist mores, enjoying being the object of desire of every passing Frenchman. I remembered a story my mother told me at a time in England just after the war. There was apparently a run on a book entitled "What every married woman should know." It was eagerly anticipated by girls, like her, who had been brought up in a Victorian atmosphere where the word sex was never even mentioned, let alone written about. However, imagine the disappointment on eagerly opening the book to find that all it was was a book on cookery and how to manage the home!

In striking contrast, here in modern-day France all the lingerie stores sell matching bra and thong sets as standard, no Frenchwoman worth her salt feeling dressed without the fillip of wearing expensive, desirable silk underwear. Irrespective of what is worn on the outside, the inner confidence that comes from wearing silk matching underwear is undeniably evident on the self-confident faces of so many Parisians. They like nothing better than to flirt at every opportunity, every girl progressively practising her art to a state of perfection as she matures. For a Frenchman to have a mistress is in itself a status symbol, the absence of which leads to many question marks about his virility, so it is said. The story goes that when a widowed man marries his mistress, this then creates a vacancy!

And French women, too, seem to think it's *comme d'habitude* to seek lovers, the very act confirming her desirability on the world's stage. I have certainly noted that French men think they're God's gift to women and often seem steeped in a permanent state of unbridled eroticism.

Could it be, though, that a Frenchman in bed is in truth rather like the French navy: relying much on hearsay, tradition, pomp and ceremony, but when the chips are down, never comes when needed!!

27
Was it all worth it?

Non, rien de rien
Non je ne regrette rien
C'est payé, balayé, oublié,
Je ne fous du passé

Avec mes souvenirs
J'ai allumé le feu
Mes chagrins, mes plaisirs
Je n'ai plus besoin d'eux

From *Je ne regrette rien*
Sung and made famous by Edith Piaf

As H and I sit relaxing on our patio, watching the sun setting low to the west, we reflect on how we ourselves have changed since making that life-enhancing move to France. As the light slowly fades and the wide, domed sky reflects the luminescence from the earth, we sit and contemplate our new lives.

Retirement is an emotive word. It's that time when we reach another 'fork' in the tree of life. Everyone as they reach that stage must ask of themselves the same question. What do we do — do we carry on as before, making do on a dwindling income supply or do we make a life-changing decision whilst we still have breath in our lungs and blood in our veins? I had often thought that there are many books and self-help programmes for dealing with all those young stages of life: Dr. Spock books on how to bring up baby, how to manage your sex-life, even how to deal with marriage and divorce. But, where are the books instructing us on how to be old?

The bible tells us that as *homo sapiens* we have long been a nomadic people, either being forced from our temporary homes by a hostile dictator or moving from country to country in search of that elusive manna from heaven. Life has a habit, though, of springing decisions upon us, sometimes when we least expect them.

In present-day England the easy option for us would have been to stay in the community we knew, enjoying the friendships built up over the years, secure in the knowledge of comforting facilities near to hand and familiar surroundings in which to work and play. But, did I want to become one of those old dears in the High Street of our homeland, with that archetypical blue-rinse and tartan trolley, trudging my relentless way through my relentless English life? No, *absolument*, non!

But that retirement 'fork' in the tree of life was fast approaching and with it, the economic decision on how to down-size to top-up our pension income. Anyone familiar with the property markets in recent years in any large English city knew that that decision is hardly worth the effort economically. So, we had looked further afield.

The US was certainly worth investigating in the first instance. Our daughter lives there and the property market is cheap and plentiful. However, visas are difficult (if nigh on impossible) to get and the all-important health insurance for immigrants of pensionable age would take up most of the benefits gained from downsizing.

So, right or wrong, here we are in the South of France! As a poor traveller it did not require a plane or sea journey, and all our belongings could be brought down by road. The long hours of sunshine and the wonderful quality of light that inspired such Impressionist painters as Degas and Renoir are now available to counter my previous SAD condition (seasonal affectation disorder) acquired from living in cold, dark northern climes. My French is holding up well, and we now have the sort of surroundings we could only have dreamed of: land in which to grow vegetables and fruit, cicadas and birds singing in the hedgerows and plenty of space between us and our village neighbours. Of course we know that France is not a panacea for all evils: there are global worries here as well as in all other countries. But, if all goes awry, it is not so far away that we couldn't return if necessary.

However, in the dying hours of daylight as we watch *les hirondelles* swooping low, diving into the permanently open windows of our garage to feed their young chirruping in their nests high up in the eaves, before swooping down to take a gulp of our deliciously cool swimming pool water, we can't believe our good fortune. We now have permanent summer sunshine, free at point of delivery, to warm our ageing bones, there is room to move, room to breathe and straight clear roads in which to enjoy touring the surrounding countryside. Additionally we have the benefit of modern technology in the form of email and Sky TV/Radio, to keep us in touch with all things British.

One of the added benefits is the joy of discovering new places. Toulouse is our nearest large international city. It is known as the *Ville Rose* (Pink City) because of its distinctive brickwork, washed over each evening by the glorious rays of the setting sun. Above the red tiled roofs necks strain to see a distant heaven underneath a panoply of blue sky, unbesmirched by air pollution or the greyness of more northern climes. Its sporting heritage boasts a highly respected rugby union team *Stade Toulousain*, which has been a four-time finalist and three-time winner in Europe's top club competition in the sport, the Heineken Cup. The city also has a rugby league team, *Toulouse Olympique*, who have won the French championship on four occasions. Don't visit on match days, though, as the traffic chaos around the stadium is legendary. (Oh, and post-World-Cup, with memories of Zidane's disgrace – don't even think of mentioning football).

Art historians tell us that Toulouse was the home of Antoine de Saint-Exupery (1904-1944), who was famous for his book *Le Petit Prince* (The Little Prince). There is a permanent gallery with numerous photos and some of his works located in the *Hotel du Grand Balcon* - just off the *Place du Capitole* - where he stayed. However, the Bohemian painter Henri de Toulouse-Lautrec never lived in Toulouse. He actually lived in Paris and shared only his name with Toulouse the city.

For as long as I can remember, and probably many years before I was born, the city planners of our home town had argued over the possibility of introducing a metro system underneath the city. They should come and look at the transport system in Toulouse. It was noticeable on a busy weekday lunchtime that the bus-lanes, so long a hot topic back home, seemed to work well simply by running in an opposite direction to the car traffic. We are, of course, newcomers and have not had the opportunity to hear any comments from the older *Toulousaines* themselves. However, from our new perspective, we looked at one of the main city-centre routes. The bus-lanes are sited each side of the road, but the long single-decker buses travel in the opposite direction to the one-way car traffic. This way, all the cars, whether in the slow or fast lanes, could easily see the oncoming buses in the lanes alongside of them.

In addition to an extensive bus system, Toulouse has a modern metro system. The VAL (Véhicule Automatique Léger) metro system is made up of driverless (automatic) rubber-tyred trains. The existing line A runs for 12.5km. It was recently extended and now runs from Balma-Gramont to Basso Cambo. The new line B, expected to open later in 2007 will add twenty stations and will intersect line A at Jean Jaurès. Line E (a tramway) is going to be done in 2009, and will roll from Beauzelles to Arènes. Line C exists since line A is the standard railway line with SNCF trains. It connects to line A at Arènes. Another oft-used commuter train line (D) runs to the city of Muret. In all, a wonderful city which we intend to visit again and again (Bruno willing!).

One of our favourite pastimes, now that we have time to stop and stare, is to look at the French as individuals. Are they essentially the same as the British, or has their wonderful climate over the centuries reaped subtle differences in their behaviour as compared to those of more northern climes? Let's take a totally biased look at what we have found over the last few years. The typical French person is a hypochondriac, a suicidal driver, cultured, flirtatious, racist(!), unhygienic, anti-American, a gourmand, sensuous, chauvinistic, chic, patriotic, proud, nationalistic, debauched, elegant, relaxed, completely unprudish about baring their bodies anywhere (particularly men seen everywhere urinating at the side of the road), philosophical, unsqueamish, superior in their attitudes to other nations, unsporting and bureaucratic.

We have discovered that living amongst the French is a considerably traumatic experience, sometimes evoking quite shocking attitudes. One busy day, in the height of the tourist season, we were doing our regular weekly shop in a small, local supermarket. Fully stocked-up, we approached the check-out to discover a seasonal long queue. We settled down to wait with typical English patience, but were irritated by a French lady ahead of us who continually left her trolley to search for forgotten items. As the check-out girl looked to us as the next person in line, we made a quick decision, not wanting to inconvenience the long lines behind us and moved the personless trolley ahead of us to one side. Two minutes later the errant French lady returned, only to lambast us, in broken pigeon-English, that "it is not the French way!" I refused to be browbeaten, so responded icily in French: "c'était nécessaire pour faire un décision…vous n'étiez pas là." We had to make a decision because you weren't there.

"Bouff," was the reply, but I could see that the people in the queue were nodding at me in agreement, so I attempted to defuse the situation into *une entente cordiale* by saying to one and all in earshot: "les hommes, on le sait bien que ils n'ont pas la patience…." All the women agreed with this truism: men everywhere were famous for their impatience in shopping situations, and H himself was unlikely to understand the depths to which I had sunk in trying to redeem the situation.

Recently I have taken to reading the local French newspapers to try and get to grips with *le savoir faire*. The use of vous or tu was recently in the news when President Sarkozy was first inaugurated in the French national elections. To which thought H, quick as a flash (as is his wont) said: "I have heard that one candidate in the forthcoming elections is called Monsieur Le Pen. Is the female candidate standing against him called Madame Le Biro?"

There was much in the newspapers of M. Sarkozy asking the departing President Chirac whether he should use tu when addressing him, to which M. Chirac allegedly replied: "quand vous voulez", as you wish, pertinently using the 'vous' form. The grammar books tell you to always use 'vous' when addressing a stranger or someone in authority, and to use 'tu' when talking to children, members of your own family or God – to whom presumably you wish to set up a personal line of communication. H, in particular, should make sure that once he has established the correct kissing regime with unfamiliar females, he doesn't fall into the trap of using 'tu', as this would indicate a more intimate relationship!

When conversing with *les françaises,* it is important to remember which topics of conversation to be handled with care. The French do not like to discuss anything that alludes to how much they earn — that is a major *faux pas* — so it's much safer to stick to topics like food and drink.

We had read that the French are known for their insularity, even worse than the Japanese and generally are impatient with foreigners. But we understood that at least the English are not the butt of their few jokes, these being reserved for the Swiss and the Belgians, whom they poke fun at due to probable jealousy over their superior cultural heritage and more refined French accents. Of course they have the humiliating memories of having to call on British and American intervention in two world wars, something they would prefer to forget. To the average Frenchman, every setback is seen as part of an international conspiracy, undoubtedly concocted by *les ros bifs*, to rob France of its jobs, culture, farms, identity and language. Look how Jacques Chirac complained about the creeping US influence on his beautiful language. We now have *le weekend*, *le fast food*, *le rambo* to name but a few.

As we have found to our cost, bureaucracy is everywhere. When one reads that the EU was actually invented by a Frenchman (Jean Monnet), it should cause no surprise as the EU is considered one of the most dictatorial and bureaucratic institutions in the world. But for me, I have developed a growing acceptance of the EU. Fundamentally, since its inception it has been proven to be the only thing across all the centuries that has actually stopped the countries of Europe from fighting each other.

The French language has reached the pinnacle of divinity in France: it is the language of love, food and the Gods, so therefore there is naturally no need to speak any other inferior tongue. The French often profess not to speak English, for example, because they would rather not exhibit their faults to all and sundry. However, this is usually a sign that they would not speak a language which to their minds has caused the decline of their great true language and even of the French empire. For ourselves, though, we have found that the locals in our village were so pleased that we had actually made an effort to speak their language. Despite our great age and length of time since we had learned it at school, they could see that we were really trying to become integrated into their wonderful way of life and so they welcomed us, if not with open arms, with considerable warmth and bonhomie.

Naturally this chronicle would not be complete without mentioning a subject which, along with sex, is dear to every French person's heart: food. They proclaim food as a French invention, along with taxes, *le guillotine* and sex, and to be *un gourmand* is the national pastime. The French will eat anything breathing that moves, swims, crawls or flies, so long as they can throw a tasty sauce over it. They don't seem to mind the horrible bits that people of more civilised sensibilities discard such as brains, entrails, hoofs and reproductive organs, and will readily enjoy frogs' legs, snails and oysters eaten alive. H and I can't seem to understand the national attitude to animals in general. On the one hand, wherever we go, people stop to pat Bruno's head and coo: "Ah, il est mignon," but then ignore regular cruelties such as animals caged in pens all-day, or animals cooked alive in boiling water.

National hypochondria is often exemplified by the standard treatment for *un crise de foie* or liver crisis usually caused by their love of prolific amounts of alcohol. *H: are you listening?* Doctors everywhere proscribe the regular(!) suppository for all such cases as well as for every other ailment under the sun, ranging from the common cold to a full-blown heart attack. Of course, the average prudish English person, as with the ubiquitous French *bidet*, would never stoop so low as to actually use it!

Someone once said that the mark of a great country is that it never breeds indifference. Indifference equals invisibility, and France is nothing if not highly visible in every field. The French enjoy what many believe to be the highest quality of life in the world, and who are we to counter that?

I took the opportunity one morning whilst H and Bruno were doing other things to wander into a house of prayer. Subconsciously I needed time to think and reflect on all these changes we had so precipitously made. After the luminescence and heat of the outside pavements, the interior was quiet and chilled. Old stone pillars preceded the ancient stone portals, which creaked slightly as I crept in. Underfoot, ancient chipped marble gave way to creaky wooden floorboards in the dim vestibule. I covered my head with a scarf and made my way forwards. The hum of chanting led me towards the main prayer hall, suddenly illuminated way above my head by a spectacular, many-branched chandelier. I found the women's section and sidled along an old wooden pew, behind a wickerwork *mechitza* screen. On either side of the prayer hall were a sprinkling of little old men, their shoulders shrouded in white and blue *tallis* shawls. They appeared to be each in their own spiritual world, rocking and chanting to the ancient *selichot* morning prayers. I looked around me, my eyes lifting to a magnificent stained-glass window. A sudden shaft of luminescent light let in a glowing lozenge of colour, illuminating and sparkling on Moses as he shouldered the enormous burden of the ten commandments from the Mount.

Although I felt much inner guilt that throughout my life I had not made more effort to understand the words of the ancient prayers, written in another time, in another ancient language, nevertheless I felt a sublime peace settle around me. For some reason I recalled the words back in England that I had uttered on leaving my place of work: It's not the outer appearances of this modern world that matter, but what's in your individual heart and soul. It was as if a voice was speaking to me, directly into the inner recesses of my brain: whatever happens, always do the right thing.

I wandered out feeling spiritually cleansed, the ancient prayers having somehow resolved within me the questions that needed answering. I hardly noticed my route homewards, my thoughts deep and close to my heart.

Back at home, as the evening draws to a close, H and I sit and reflect as we watch our nightly entertainment: the evening 'bird' show. Where else in the world could we expect to see a charm of fifty goldfinches all feeding together at our specially-erected bird table? We have several tables, each placed in different locations around the garden in order to give smaller or more timid birds a chance to feed. On evenings when there is a large collection of birds feeding on our sunflower, *tournesol*, seeds, it is often the case that the tits will queue up on nearby branches for a turn. We have some feeders with a large opening at the base, which give the blue tits the chance to sneak a seed whilst the pretty but aggressive goldfinch is lording the roost.

We were advised that for those of us who enjoy feeding wild birds in the winter, peanuts, sunflower seeds and plenty of fat are the most important foodstuffs, providing the proteins and energy the birds need so much. We were told never to put out salted or artificially-flavoured foods or give linseeds as these contain a chemical the birds' digestive systems can't cope with. And, once you start to feed wild birds, it is a lifetime's habit because once a wild bird is dependent on the food provided it will die if you stop feeding

It is not unusual during the winter months to see goldfinches (*chardonneret élégant*), blackbirds, robins, collared doves, great, blue and coal tits, sparrows, greenfinches (*verdier*), hawfinches (*grosbec*), serins, bullfinches, siskins and bramblings all hovering low over our swimming pool.

The common buzzards who nest in our region in the summer fly south during the winter months to seek more warmth in southern Spain or north Africa, whilst in the winter we see birds taking their place who have flown all those miles south from northern European countries like Lithuania or Norway. It is a constantly changing scene. Local short-toed eagles have even been seen eating snakes in the grass, leading H to observe that it's a good job that certain politicians don't come to this area very often….

As the darkness descends all around us, we crane our necks back and look at the wondrous nightly show of trillions of stars, some distant, some near, but all twinkling, pirouetting and turning in the clear, velvety-black sky. What is this life telling us? Surely, the message is that we mere humans are but tiny , inconsequential, varieties of matter. None of us know the reason for our existence. In philosophical mood, we turn our minds to what we have done in our lives. Was it a moral duty for the two of us to leave the place where we had lived all our lives to move to a place where the living would be easier? Was it the right thing for us to weigh up the consequences and choose the best option for us that would cause the least pain or discomfort to others ?

So, how can we differentiate between our 'moral duty' and what is merely advice that we can discard if we wish ? People have often thought of their moral obligations as being obligations to a person even when no other human is apparently involved. This is where the concept of conscience comes in. It appears as a tiny voice inside our heads forcing us into a certain action, reminding us if we haven't yet done it, and even telling us off if we should be so foolish as not to do it.

Conscience seems to be intimately connected with our most innermost emotions: especially guilt, fear, self-reproach, shame and remorse. I can certainly empathise with that. It is essentially brought forth when we feel regret after doing something apparently wrong. Conversely, those who feel shame are those who are concerned at how they appear to others and what others might think of them. So, it follows that if we let our conscience lead us 'by the nose', then it could make us follow an incorrect path, rather than allowing us to use our freewill to choose what is right and wrong and act accordingly.

Was moving to France then the correct or the wrong path, one that we selfishly chose above all other things? Or was it, as P. J. Mill famously put it: all right as long as no harm was done to others?

As we continued to stare at the myriad, ever-changing kaleidoscope of the star-spangled heavens, we somehow came to a realisation that answered my personal question: what of my inherited negativity? Has this experiment of moving our lives to France made a difference to my personal outlook on life? H used to joke that my blood group should 'be negative'. But now, was I any different as a result of all that had happened to us in France?

The answer, shouting down loud and clear from the heavens was:

"Yes, yes, yes!"

The combination of the quality of the light (*la qualité de la lumière*), the amazing *belle cuisine*, the open spaces, fresh air and the slower lifestyle of French rural village life have fused together to do what England could never do for me: change a natural-born pessimist into one who now enjoys life to the full. It reminds me of my rose-tinted memories of

England fifty years ago, but without all the anguish and postwar ration books. No more licking those infernally irritating stamps of life.

Well done, France.

We have come to a decision. We are here to stay.

*Vive la France. Vive les français. Vive la diff*érence!

Afterword

This story was pretty much an autobiographical account of how, at the advanced age of approaching retirement, my husband and I became so embroiled, enmeshed and tangled in the minutiae of life in England that we made the outrageous decision to move away from everything we had known to a totally new life abroad. It is a no-holds barred, true story exactly how it happened.

All the events chronicled within actually happened, but certain names have been changed. The name of the French village where we lived has been altered to protect the identities of the residents, and the names of individuals mentioned within have also been changed.

Similarly, the scenes depicted in our life in England before we moved abroad are also absolutely true, but again the exact town has not been revealed, nor have the identities of the people with whom we worked nor workplace names been revealed, named or disclosed.

You can read all the books in the world, but nothing (and I mean, nothing) can prepare you for experiencing life in the raw in a new country, especially not at our grand old age.

Of course, the essential thing to bear in mind is that it's absolutely no use moving to a country like France with your 'English head' on, so to speak. That's indubitably the route to disaster. Let"s face it: the French aren't like us. It's not just the berets and garlic. They have a completely different outlook and way of doing things. English mindsets have grown up from a lifetime of living with other Englishmen. We have suffered long and hard over the vagaries of English workmen, office colleagues, etc. And we know all about the English media and its fetish for hysteria, intrigue, bad news and scandal.

But French life is simply foreign, isn't it? Well yes, but now that we have learned to look at things through their eyes, nothing will ever be the same again.

This adventure all began in 2005. It is now 2017. Could it be that we would ever envisage a return to England? What on Earth would persuade us to do that? Look out for the sequel – coming soon!

Olga Swan
Summer 2017

Fantastic Books
Great Authors

CROOKED CAT

Meet our authors and discover
our exciting range:

- Gripping Thrillers
- Cosy Mysteries
- Romantic Chick-Lit
- Fascinating Historicals
- Exciting Fantasy
- Young Adult and Children's Adventures
- Non-Fiction

Visit us at:
www.crookedcatbooks.com

Join us on facebook:
www.facebook.com/realcrookedcat

Printed in Great Britain
by Amazon